George Bruce Malleson

Akbar and the rise of the Mughal empire

George Bruce Malleson

Akbar and the rise of the Mughal empire

ISBN/EAN: 9783337274375

Printed in Europe, USA, Canada, Australia, Japan

Cover: Foto ©ninafisch / pixelio.de

More available books at **www.hansebooks.com**

RULERS OF INDIA

Akbar

AND THE RISE OF THE MUGHAL EMPIRE

By COLONEL G. B. MALLESON, C.S.I.

FIFTH THOUSAND

Oxford
AT THE CLARENDON PRESS: 1896

CONTENTS

CHAP.		PAGES
I.	The Argument	5-11
II.	The Family and Early Days of Bábar	12-16
III.	Bábar conquers Kábul	17-25
IV.	Bábar's Invasions of India	26-34
V.	The Position of Bábar in Hindustán	35-49
VI.	Humáyún and the Early Days of Akbar	50-59
VII.	Humáyún invades India. His Death	60-64
VIII.	Akbar's Fight for his Father's Throne	65-71
IX.	General Condition of India in the Middle of the Sixteenth Century	72-80
X.	The Tutelage under Bairám Khán	81-90
XI.	Chronicle of the Reign	91-145
XII.	The Principles and Internal Administration of Akbar	146-200
	Index	201-204

NOTE

The orthography of proper names follows the system adopted by the Indian Government for the *Imperial Gazetteer of India*. That system, while adhering to the popular spelling of very well-known places, such as Punjab, Lucknow, etc., employs in all other cases the vowels with the following uniform sounds:—

a, as in woman: *á*, as in land: *i*, as in police: *i*, as in intr*i*gue: *o*, as in cold: *u*, as in bull: *ú*, as in sure: *e*, as in grey.

HENRY MORSE STEPHENS

THE EMPEROR AKBAR

CHAPTER I

THE ARGUMENT

I CRAVE the indulgence of the reader whilst I explain as briefly as possible the plan upon which I have written this short life of the great sovereign who firmly established the Mughal dynasty in India[1].

The original conception of such an empire was not Akbar's own. His grandfather, Bábar, had conquered a great portion of India, but during the five years which elapsed between the conquest and his death, Bábar enjoyed but few opportunities of donning the robe of the administrator. By the rivals whom he had overthrown and by the children of the soil, Bábar was alike regarded as a conqueror, and as nothing more. A man of remarkable ability, who had spent all his life in arms, he was really an adventurer, though a brilliant adventurer, who, soaring above his contemporaries in genius, taught in the rough school of adversity, had beheld from his eyrie at Kábul the distracted condition

[1] For the purposes of this sketch I have referred to the following authorities: *Memoirs of Bábar*, written by himself, and translated by Leyden and Erskine; Erskine's *Bábar and Humáyún*; *The Ain-i-Akbari* (Blochmann's translation); *The History of India, as told by its own Historians*, edited from the posthumous papers of Sir H. M. Elliot, K.C.B., by Professor Dowson; Dow's *Ferishta*; Elphinstone's *History of India*; Tod's *Annals of Rajast'han*, and various other works.

of fertile Hindustán, and had dashed down upon her plains with a force that was irresistible. Such was Bábar, a man greatly in advance of his age, generous, affectionate, lofty in his views, yet, in his connection with Hindustán, but little more than a conqueror. He had no time to think of any other system of administration than the system with which he had been familiar all his life, and which had been the system introduced by his Afghán predecessors into India, the system of governing by means of large camps, each commanded by a general devoted to himself, and each occupying a central position in a province. It is a question whether the central idea of Bábar's policy was not the creation of an empire in Central Asia rather than of an empire in India.

Into this system the welfare of the children of the soil did not enter. Possibly, if Bábar had lived, and had lived in the enjoyment of his great abilities, he might have come to see, as his grandson saw, that such a system was practically unsound; that it was wanting in the great principle of cohesion, of uniting the interests of the conquering and the conquered; that it secured no attachment, and conciliated no prejudices; that it remained, without roots, exposed to all the storms of fortune. We, who know Bábar by his memoirs, in which he unfolds the secrets of his heart, confesses all his faults, and details all his ambitions, may think that he might have done this if he had had the opportunity. But the opportunity was denied to him. The time between the first battle of Pánípat, which gave him the north-western provinces of India, and his death, was too short to allow him to think of much more than the securing of his conquests, and the adding to them of additional provinces. He entered India a conqueror. He remained a conqueror, and nothing more, during the five years he ruled at Agra.

His son, Humáyún, was not qualified by nature to perform the task which Bábar had been obliged to neglect. His character, flighty and unstable, and his abilities, wanting in the constructive faculty, alike unfitted him for the duty. He ruled eight years in India without contributing a single stone to the foundation of an empire that was to remain. When, at the end of that period, his empire fell, as had fallen the kingdoms of his Afghán predecessors, and from the same cause, the absence of any roots in the soil, the result of a single defeat in the field, he lost at one blow all that Bábar had gained south of the Indus. India disappeared, apparently for ever, from the grasp of the Mughal.

The son of Bábar had succumbed to an abler general, and that abler general had at once completely supplanted him. Fortunately for the Mughal, more fortunately still for the people of India, that abler general, though a man of great ability, had inherited views not differing in any one degree from those of the Afghán chiefs who had preceded him in the art of establishing a dynasty. The conciliation of the millions of Hindustán did not enter into his system. He, too, was content to govern by camps located in the districts he had conquered. The consequence was that when he died other men rose to compete for the empire. The confusion rose in the course of a few years to such a height, that in 1554, just fourteen years after he had fled from the field of Kanauj, Humáyún recrossed the Indus, and recovered Northern India. He was still young, but still as incapable of founding a stable empire as when he succeeded his father.

He left behind him writings which prove that, had his life been spared, he would still have tried to govern on the old plan which had broken in the hands of so many conquerors who had gone before him, and in his own. Just before his death he drew up a system for the administration of India. It was the old system of separate camps in a fixed centre, each independent of the other, but all supervised by the Emperor. It was an excellent plan, doubtless, for securing conquered provinces, but it was absolutely deficient in any scheme for welding the several provinces and their people into one harmonious whole.

The accident which deprived Humáyún of his life before the second battle of Pánípat had bestowed upon the young Akbar, then a boy of fourteen, the succession to the empire of Bábar, was, then, in every sense, fortunate for Hindustán. Humáyún, during his long absence, his many years of striving with fortune, had learnt nothing and had forgotten nothing. The boy who succeeded him, and who, although of tender years, had already had as many adventures, had seen as many vicissitudes of fortune, as would fill the life of an ordinary man, was untried. He had indeed by his side a man who was esteemed the greatest general of that period, but whose mode of governing had been formed in the rough school of the father of his pupil. This boy, however, possessed, amid other great talents, the genius of construction. During the few years that he allowed his famous general to govern in his name, he pondered deeply over the causes which had rendered evanescent all the preceding dynasties, which had prevented them from taking root in the soil. When he had matured his plans, he took the government into his own hands, and founded a dynasty which flourished so long as it adhered to his system, and which began to decay only when it departed from one of its main principles, the principle of toleration and conciliation.

I trust that in the preceding summary I have made it clear to the reader that whilst, in a certain sense, Bábar was the founder of the Mughal dynasty in India, he transmitted to his successor only the idea of the mere conqueror. Certainly Humáyún inherited only that idea, and associating it with no other, lost what his father had won. It is true that he ultimately regained a portion of it, but still as a mere conqueror. It was the grandson who struck into the soil the roots which took a firm hold of it, sprung up, and bore rich and abundant fruit in the happiness and contentment of the conquered races.

This is the argument to the development of which I have devoted the following pages. The book seems to me naturally to divide itself into three parts. To Bábar, as the developer of the idea of the invasion and conquest of India, I have devoted the first part. He was a remarkable man, and he would have been remarkable in any age. When he died, at the early age of forty-eight, he left behind him a record which may be read with interest and profit even at the close of this nineteenth century. It has seemed to me the more necessary to devote a considerable space to him inasmuch as the reader will not fail to discern, in the actions of the grandson, the spirit and energy and innate nobility of character of the grandfather. Of Humáyún, whose life properly belongs to the first part, I have written as much only as seemed to me necessary to illustrate the cause of his fall, and to describe the early days of the hero of the book, who was born in Sind, during the father's flight from India.

The remaining two-thirds of the book have been given to Akbar. But, here again, I have subdivided the subject. In the first of the two-thirds, I have narrated, from the pages and on the authority of contemporary Muhammadan historians, the political events of the reign. In the last chapter I have endeavoured to paint the man. From the basis of the records of the Ain-í-Akbarí and other works I have tried to show what he was as an administrator, as an organiser, as the promulgator of a system which we English have to a great extent inherited, as a conciliator of differences which had lasted through five hundred years, of prejudices which had lived for all time. I have described him as a husband, as a father, as a man, who, despite of a religious education abounding in the inculcation of hostility to all who differed from him, gave his intellect the freest course, and based his conduct on the teachings of his intellect. This chapter, I am free to confess, constitutes the most interesting portion of the book. For the sake of it, I must ask the reader to pardon me for inflicting upon him that which precedes it.

CHAPTER II

THE FAMILY AND EARLY DAYS OF BÁBAR

ON the 9th of April, 1336, there was born to the chief of the Birbás, a tribe of the purest Mughal origin, at Shehr-Sebz, thirty miles to the north of Samarkand, a son, the eldest of his family. This boy, who was called Taimur, and who was descended in the female line from Chengiz Khán, was gifted by nature with the qualities which enable a man to control his fellow men. Fortune gave him the chance to employ those qualities to the best advantage. The successors of Chengiz Khán in the male line had gradually sunk into feebleness and sloth, and, in 1370, the family in that line had died out. Taimur, then thirty-four, seized the vacated seat, gained, after many vicissitudes of fortune, the complete upper hand, and established himself at Samarkand the undisputed ruler of all the country between the Oxus and the Jaxartes. Then he entered upon that career of conquest which terminated only with his life. He established his authority in Mughalistán, or the country between the Tibet mountains, the Indus and Mekrán, to the south, and Siberia to the north; in Kipchak, the country lying north of the lower course of the Jaxartes, the sea of Aral, and the Caspian, including the rich lands on the Don and Wolga, and part of those on the Euxine; he conquered India, and forced the people of territories between the Dardanelles and Delhi to acknowledge his supremacy. When he died, on the 18th February, 1405, he left behind him one of the greatest empires the world has ever seen.

After his death his empire rapidly broke up, and although it was partly reconstituted by his great-grandson, Abusáid, the death of this prince in 1469, when surprised in the defiles of the mountains near Ardebil, and the defeat of his army, precipitated a fresh division among his sons. To the third of these, Umershaikh Mirzá, was assigned the province of Ferghaná, known also, from the name of its capital, as Khokand.

Umershaikh was the father of Bábar. He was an ambitious man, bent on increasing his dominions. But the other members of his family were actuated by a like ambition, and when he died from the effects of an accident, in 1494, he was actually besieged in Akhsí, a fortress-castle which he had made his capital.

His eldest son, Bábar, then just twelve years old, was at the time at Andiján, thirty-six miles from Akhsí. The enemy was advancing on Andiján. Bábar, the day following his father's death (June 9), seized the citadel, and opened negotiations with the invader. His efforts would have availed him little, if there had not existed jealousies and divisions in the hostile camp. These worked for him so as to secure to him all that remained of Ferghána. But he had lost the important towns of Khojend, Marghinan, and Uratiupé.

For two years after the retirement of the invader, the boy rested, consolidating his resources, and watching his opportunity. Then, troubles having arisen in Samarkand, he made a dash at that city, then the most important in Central Asia. He forced its surrender (November, 1497), but as he would not allow his troops to pillage, these deserted him by thousands. He held on, however, until the news that Ferghána was invaded compelled him to quit his hold. On the eve of his departure he was prostrated by a severe illness, and when at length he reached Ferghána it was to hear that his capital had surrendered to his enemies. He was, in fact, a king without a kingdom. 'To save Andijan,' he wrote, 'I had given up Samarkand: and now I found that I had lost the one without preserving the other.'

He persevered, however, recovered Ferghána, though a Ferghána somewhat shorn of its proportions, and once more made a dash at Samarkand. The Uzbeks, however, forced him to raise the siege, and, his own dominions having in the interval been overrun and conquered, he fell back in the direction of Kesh, his birthplace. After many adventures and strivings with fortune, he resolved with the aid of the very few adherents who remained to him, to return and attempt the surprise of Samarkand. It was a very daring venture, for his entire following numbered but two hundred and forty men. He made the attempt, was foiled; renewed it, and succeeded. He was but just in time. For the last of the garrison had but just yielded, when the chief of the Uzbeks was seen riding hard for the place, at the head of the vanguard of his army. He had to retire, baffled.

But Bábar could not keep his conquest. The following spring the Uzbeks returned in force. To foil them Bábar took up a very strong position outside the city, on the Bokhára road, his right flank covered by the river Kohik. Had he been content to await his enemy in this position, he would probably have compelled him to retire, for it was too strong to be forced. But he was induced by the astrologers, against his own judgment, to advance beyond it to attack the Uzbek army. In the battle which followed, and which he almost won, he was eventually beaten, and retreated within the walls of the city. Here he maintained himself for five months, but had then to succumb to famine. He was allowed to quit the city with his following, and made his way, first to Uratiupé, ultimately to Dehkát, a village assigned to him by the reigning Khán of the former place. For three years that followed he lived the life of an adventurer: now an exile in the desert; now marching and gaining a throne; always joyous; always buoyed up by hope of ultimate success; always acting with energy and vigour. He attempted to win back, and had been forced to abandon, Ferghánâ: then he resolved, with a motley band of two to three hundred men, to march on Khorásán. It seemed madness, but the madness had a method. How he marched, and what was the result of his march, will be told in the next chapter.

CHAPTER III

Bábar conquers Kábul

AT this period the kingdom of Kábul comprehended solely the provinces of Kábul and Ghazní, the territory which we should call Eastern Afghánistán. Herát was the capital of an independent empire, at this time the greatest in Central Asia; and Kandahár, Bajáur, Swát, and Pesháwar, were ruled by chiefs who had no connection with Kábul. The tribes of the plains and outlying valleys alone acknowledged the authority of the King of that country. The clans of the mountains were as independent and refractory as their descendants were up to a recent period. Kábul at this time was in a state bordering upon anarchy. The late King, Abdul-rizák, a grandson of the Abusáid referred to in the preceding chapter, had been surprised in, and driven from, the city, by Muhammad Mokim, a son of the ruler of Kandahár, and that prince, taking no thought of the morrow, was reigning as though all the world were at peace, and he at least were free from danger.

Bábar, I have said, tired of his wandering life, had resolved to march on Khorásán. He crossed the Oxus, therefore, and joined by Bákí, the son of Sultán

Khusrou, ruler of the country, marched on Ajer, remained there a few days; then, hearing that the Mughals in Khusrou's service had revolted, he marched towards Talikán, so as to be able to take advantage of the situation. Between the two places he was joined by the Mughals in question, and learnt that Sultán Khusrou, with the remainder of his troops, was on his way to Kábul. The two armies were so close to one another, that an interview took place between the leaders, which resulted in the complete submission of Khusrou, whose troops came over in crowds to Bábar. Thus strengthened, Bábar marched upon Kábul, besieged it, and took it (October, 1504). By this sudden change of fortune, he found himself all at once King of Kábul and Ghazní, a kingdom far more powerful than the Ferghání which he had inherited and lost.

Bábar had but just begun to feel his seat in his new kingdom when he received an invitation to invade a district called Bhera, south of the river Jehlam, and therefore within the borders of India. The invitation was too agreeable to his wishes to be refused, and he accordingly set out for Jalálábád. The time was January, 1505. The Sultán—for so he was styled—records in his journals the impression produced upon him by the first sight of that favoured part of Asia, an impression shared, doubtless, by his successors in the path of invasion, and which may well account for their determination to push on. 'I had never before,' he wrote, 'seen warm countries nor the country of

Hindustán. On reaching them, I all at once saw a new world; the vegetables, the plants, the trees, the wild animals, all were different. I was struck with astonishment, and indeed there was room for wonder.' He then proceeded by the Khaibar Pass to Peshawar, and, not crossing the Indus, marched by Kohát, Bangash, Banú, and Desht Daman, to Múltán. Thence he followed the course of the Indus for a few days, then turned westward, and returned to Kábul by way of Chotiáli and Ghazní. The expedition has been called Bábar's first invasion of India, but as he only touched the fringes of the country, it took rather the character of a reconnoitring movement. Such as it was, it filled him with an earnest desire to take an early opportunity to see more.

But, like every other conqueror who has been attracted by India, he deemed it of vital importance to secure himself in the first place of Kandahár. Internal troubles for a time delayed the expedition. Then, when these had been appeased, external events came to demand his attention. His old enemy, Shaibání, was once more ruling at Samarkand, and, after some lesser conquests, had come to lay siege to Balkh. Sultán Husen Mirzá of Herát, alarmed at his progress, sent at once a messenger to Bábar to aid him in an attack on the invader. Bábar at once responded, and setting out from Kábul in June, 1506, reached Kahmerd, and halted there to collect and store supplies. He was engaged in this work when the information was brought him by a messenger that

Sultán Husen Mirzá was dead. He at once pushed on, and after a march of eight hundred miles joined the sons of the late Sultán and their army on the river Murgháb.

Two of the sons of the Sultán had succeeded him as joint-rulers. Bábar found them elegant, accomplished, and intelligent, but effeminate, devoted to pleasure, and utterly incapable of making head against the hardy Shaibání. Whilst they were pleasuring in camp, the latter had taken Balkh. After some discussion, the two kings decided to break up their army and recommence in the spring. Winter was now coming on, and Bábar was persuaded, against his better judgment, to visit his two hosts at Herát. His description of that royal city takes up pages of his autobiography[1]. For twenty days he visited every day fresh places; nor was it till the 24th of December that he decided to march homewards.

Our countrymen who served in Afghánistán during the war of 1879-81 can realise what that march must have been; how trying, how difficult, how all but impossible. The distance was twenty days' journey in summer. The road across the mountains, though not very difficult in summer, was especially trying in the depth of winter, and it was at that season, the snow falling around him, that Bábar undertook it. He himself showed the way, and with incredible exertion led the army, exhausted and reckless, to the foot of

[1] *Memoirs of Bábar*, translated by Leyden and Erskine, pp. 203-208.

the Zirín Pass. There the situation seemed hopeless. The storm was violent; the snow was deep; and the Pass was so narrow that but one person could pass at a time. Still Bábar pushed on, and at nightfall reached a cave large enough to admit a few persons. With the generosity which was a marked feature of his character he made his men enter it, whilst, shovel in hand, he dug for himself a hole in the snow, near its mouth. Meanwhile those within the cave had discovered that its proportions increased as they went further in, and that it could give shelter to fifty or sixty persons. On this Bábar entered, and shared with his men their scanty store of provisions. Next morning, the snow and tempest ceased, and the army pushed on. At length, towards the end of February, he approached Kábul, only, however, to learn that a revolt had taken place in the city, and that although his garrison was faithful, the situation was critical. Bábar was equal to the occasion. Opening communication with his partisans, by a well-executed surprise he regained the place. His treatment of the rebels was merciful in the extreme.

During the spring of that year, 1507, Shaibání Khán, the Uzbek chief, who had formerly driven Bábar from Samarkand, had attacked and taken Balkh; then invaded Khorásán and occupied Herát. Kandahár, which had been to a certain extent a dependency of the rulers of Herát, had been seized by the sons of Mír Zulnun Beg, who had been its Governor under Sultán Husen Mirzá, and these had invoked the assistance of Bábar against Shaibání. Bábar, accordingly, marched for Kandahár. On his way thither, he was joined by many of the flying adherents of the expelled House of Sultán Husen. But, before he could reach Kandahár, Shaibání Khán had put pressure on the sons of Zulnun, and these had accepted his sovereignty. They notified this act to Bábar in a manner not to be mistaken. The latter, therefore, prepared to make good his claims by force of arms.

His army was not numerous, but he had confidence in it and in himself. From Kilát-í-Ghilzaí, where he first scented the change of front at Kandahár, he had marched to the ford across the Tarnak. Thence, confirmed in his ideas, he moved in order of battle, along the course of the stream, to Bábá Walí, five or six miles to the north of Kandahár, and had occupied the hill of Kálíshad. Here he intended to rest, and sent out his foragers to collect supplies. But, soon after these had quitted the camp, he beheld the enemy's army, to the number of five thousand, move from the city towards him. He had but a thousand men under arms, the remainder being engaged in foraging, but he saw it was not a time to hesitate. Ranging his men in defensive order, he awaited the attack. That attack was led in person by the sons of Zulnun with great gallantry; but Bábar not only repulsed it, and forced the assailants to flee, but, in his pursuit, he cut them off from the city, which surrendered to him with all its treasures. The spoils of the place were magnificently rich. Bábar did not, however, remain in

Kandahár. Leaving his brother, Nasír Mirzá, to defend it, he returned to Kábul, and arrived there at the end of July (1507), as he writes, 'with much plunder and great reputation.'

Hardly had he arrived when he learned that Shaibání Khán had arrived before Kandahár and was besieging his brother there. He was puzzled how to act, for he was not strong enough to meet Shaibání in the field. A strategist by nature, he recognised at the moment that the most effective mode open to him would be to make an offensive demonstration. He doubted only whether such a demonstration should be directed against Badakshán, whence he could threaten Samarkand, or against India. Finally he decided in favour of the latter course, and, as prompt in action as he was quick in decision, he set out for the Indus, marching down the Kábul river. When, however, he had been a few days at Jalálábád, he heard that Kandahár had surrendered to Shaibání. Upon this, the object of the expedition having vanished, he returned to Kábul.

I must pass lightly over the proceedings of the next seven years, eventful though they were. In those years, from 1507 to 1514, Bábar marching northwards, recovered Ferghaná, defeated the Uzbeks, and took Bokhára and Samarkand. But the Uzbeks, returning, defeated Bábar at Kulmalik, and forced him to abandon those two cities. Attempting to recover them, he was defeated again at Ghajdewan and driven back to Hisár[1]. Finding, after a time, his chances there desperate, he returned to Kábul. This happened in the early months of 1514.

Again there was an interval of eight years, also to be passed lightly over. During that period Bábar chastised the Afgháns of the mountains, took Swát, and finally acquired Kandahár by right of treaty (1522). He took possession of, and incorporated in his dominions, that city and its dependencies, including parts of the lowlands lying chiefly along the lower course of the Helmand.

Meanwhile Sháh Beg, the eldest son of the Zulnun, who had formerly ruled in Kandahár, had marched upon and had conquered Sind, and had made Bukkur the capital. He died in June, 1524. As soon as this intelligence reached the Governor of Narsápur, Sháh Hásán, that nobleman, a devoted adherent of the family of Taimur, proclaimed Bábar ruler of the country, and caused the Khatbá, or prayer for the sovereign, to be read in his name throughout Sind. There was considerable opposition, but Sháh Hásán conquered the whole province, and governed it, acknowledging Bábar as his suzerain. At length, in 1525, he was invited to Múltán. He marched against the fortress, and, after a protracted siege, took it by storm (August or September, 1526). Meanwhile, great

[1] There are two other Hisárs famous in Eastern history: the one in India about a hundred miles north of Delhi: the other in the province of Azarbijan, in Persia, thirty-two miles from the Takht-i-Sulaimán. The Hisár referred to in the text is a city on an affluent of the Oxus, a hundred and thirty miles north-east of Balkh.

events had happened in India. On the 29th of April, of the same year, the battle of Pánípat had delivered India into the hands of Bábar. Before proceeding to narrate his invasion of that country it is necessary that I should describe, very briefly, the condition of its actual rulers at the time.

CHAPTER IV

Bábar's Invasions of India

INTO the first period of Indian history, that extending from the earliest times to the invasion of Mahmúd of Ghazní, in the beginning of the eleventh century, I do not propose to enter. The world, indeed, possesses little detailed knowledge of that period. It is known that from the Indus to Cape Comorin the country was peopled by several distinct races, speaking a variety of languages; that the prevailing religions were those of the Bráhman, the Buddhist, and the Jain; and that the wars periodically occurring between the several kings of the several provinces or divisions were mostly religious wars.

The invasion of Mahmúd of Ghazní came first, in the year 1001, to disturb the existing system. But although Mahmúd, and his successors of the Ghazní dynasty, penetrated to Delhi, to Rájpútána, and to the furthest extremities of Gujarát, they did not practically extend their permanent rule beyond the Punjab. The territories to the south-east of the Sutlej still remained subject to Hindu sovereigns. But in 1186, the dynasty of the Ghaznívís was destroyed by the dynasty of Ghor or Ghur, founded by an Afghán of Ghur, a district in Western Afghánistán, a hundred and twenty miles to the south-east of the city of Herát, on the road to Kábul. The Ghuri dynasty was, in its turn, supplanted, in 1288, by that of the Khiljí or Ghiljí. The princes of this House, after reigning with great renown for thirty-three years over Delhi and a portion of the territories now known as the North-west Provinces, and, pushing their conquests beyond the Narbadá and the Deccan, made way, in 1321, for the Tughlak dynasty, descended from Túrkí slaves. The Tughlaks did not possess the art of consolidation. During the ninety-one years of their rule the provinces ruled by their predecessors gradually separated from the central authority at Delhi. The invasion of Taimur (1388-9) dealt a fatal blow to an authority already crumbling. The chief authority lingered indeed for twelve-years in the hands of the then representative, Sultán Máhmud. It then passed for a time into the hands of a family which did not claim the royal title. This family, known in history as the Saiyid dynasty, ruled nominally in Northern India for about thirty-three years, but the rule had no coherence, and a powerful Afghán of the Lodí family took the opportunity to endeavour to concentrate power in his own hands.

The Muhammadan rule in India had indeed become by this time the rule of several disjointed chiefs over several disjointed provinces, subject in point of fact to no common head. Thus, in 1450, Delhi, with a small territory around it, was held by the representative of the Saiyid family. Within fourteen miles of the capital, Ahmad Khán ruled independently in Mewát. Sambhal, or the province now known as Rohilkhand, extending to the very walls of Delhi, was occupied by Daryá Khán Lodí. Jalesar, now the Itah district, by Isá Khán Turk: the district now known as Farukhábád by Rájá Partáb Singh: Biána by Dáúd Khán Lodí: and Lahore, Dipálpúr, and Sirhind, as far south as Pánípat, by Behlul Lodí. Múltán, Jaunpur, Bengal, Málwá, and Gujarát, each had its separate king.

Over most of these districts, and as far eastward as the country immediately to the north of Western Bihár, Behlul Lodí, known as Sultán Behlul, succeeded on the disappearance of the Saiyids in asserting his sole authority, 1450–88. His son and successor, Sultán Sikandar Lodí, subdued Behar, invaded Bengal, which, however, he subsequently agreed to yield to Allah-u-dín, its sovereign, and not to invade it again; and overran a great portion of Central India. On his death, in 1518, he had concentrated under his own rule the territories now known as the Punjab; the North-western Provinces, including Jaunpur; a great part of Central India; and Western Bihár. But, in point of fact, the concentration was little more than nominal. The Afghán nobles, to whom from necessity the Lodí Sultán committed the charge of the several districts, were indeed bound to their sovereign by a kind of feudal tenure, but within the circle of his own charge each of them made his own will absolute, and insisted on obedience to his decrees alone.

The result of this arrangement was that when Sultán Sikandar died the several important nobles, impatient even of nominal obedience, resolved, acting in concert, to assign to his son, Ibráhím, the kingdom of Delhi only, and to divide the rest of the deceased Sultán's dominions amongst themselves, Jaunpur alone excepted. This province was to be assigned to the younger brother of Ibráhím, as a separate kingdom, in subordination to Delhi. It would appear that when the proposal was first made to him, Ibráhím, probably seeing no remedy, assented. Upon the remonstrances of his kinsmen, Khán Jahán Lodí, however, he withdrew his assent and recalled his brother, who had already set out for Jaunpur. The brother refused to return. A civil war ensued in which Ibráhím was victorious. On the death of his brother, in 1518, Ibráhím endeavoured to assert his authority over his ambitious nobles. They rebelled. He quelled the rebellion. But the cruel use he made of his victory, far from quenching the discontent, caused fresh revolts. The nobles of Behar, of Oudh, of Jaunpur, flew to arms: the Punjab followed the example. The civil war was conducted with great fury and with varying fortunes on both sides. It was when the crisis was extreme that Allah-u-dín, uncle of Sultán Ibráhím, fled to the camp of Bábar, then engaged in the pacification of the Kandahár districts, and implored him to place him on the throne of Delhi. Almost simultaneously there came to the King of Kábul a still more tempting offer from Dáolát Khán, Governor of Lahore, and who was hard pressed by Ibráhím's general, begging for assistance, and offering in return to acknowledge him as his sovereign. Bábar agreed, and marched at once in the direction of Lahore.

The foregoing sketch of the internal condition of India during the five centuries which had elapsed since the invasion of Mahmúd of Ghazní will explain, I hope sufficiently clearly, how it was that none of the successive dynasties had taken root in the soil. Whether that dynasty were Ghazniví, or Ghurí, or Tughlak, or Saiyid, or Lodí, the representative had fought merely for his own hand and his own advantage. The nobles of the ruling sovereign had in this respect followed the example of their master. Hindustán had thus been overrun and partly occupied by the feudal followers of chiefs, who in turn owed feudal allegiance which they would or would not render, according to the power and capacity of the supreme lord. There had been no welding of the interest of the conquerors and the conquered such as took place in England after the Conquest. The Muhammadans sat as despotic rulers of an alien people, who obeyed them because they could not resist. There was no thought of attaching that people to the ruling dynasty either by sympathy or by closer union. The conquerors had come as aliens, and as aliens they remained. Their hold on the country was thus superficial: it had no root in the affections of the people, and it could be maintained only by the sword. It was in this respect that it differed so widely from the Mughal dynasty, as represented by Akbar, that was to succeed it.

The first invasion of India by Bábar, not reckoning the hasty visit spoken of on page 18, occurred in 1519. Some historians assert that there was a second invasion the same year. But Ferishtá is probably correct when he says that this so-called invasion amounted simply to an expedition against the Yusufzais, in the course of which Bábar advanced as far as Pesháwar, but did not cross the Indus. There is no doubt, however, that he made an expedition, called the third, in 1520. On this occasion he crossed the Indus, marched into the part known now as the Ráwal Pindí division, crossed the Jehlam, reached Siálkót, which he spared, and then marched on Saiyidpur, which he plundered. He was called from this place to Kábul to meet a threatened attack upon that capital.

The abortive result of this third expedition more than ever convinced Bábar that no invasion of Hindustán could with certainty succeed unless he could secure his base at Kandahár. He spent, therefore, the next two or three years in securing that stronghold and the territory between Ghazní and Khorásán. He had just succeeded in settling these districts on an efficient basis when he received the messages from Allah-u-dín Lodí and Dáolát Khán of Lahore, the latter of which decided him to undertake his fourth expedition to India. Once more did he cross the Indus, the

Jehlam, and the Chenáb, and advanced within ten miles of Lahore. There he was met by, and there he defeated, the army of the adherents of the House of Lodí. Lahore fell a prize to his troops. But he halted there but four days; then pushing on, reached and stormed Dipálpúr[1]. Here he was joined by Dáolát Khán and his sons. These, however, dissatisfied with the rewards meted out to them, began to intrigue against their new master. Bábar was approaching Sirhind, on his way to Delhi, when he discovered their machinations. He determined, then, to renounce for the moment his forward movement, and to return to Kábul. This he did after having parcelled out the Punjab among chiefs upon whom he hoped he could depend.

Scarcely had he crossed the Indus when the Punjab became the scene of a renewed struggle. Allah-u-dín Lodí, to whom the district of Dipálpúr had been consigned, fled in despair to Kábul, hoping that Bábar would himself undertake the invasion of India. At the moment Bábar could not comply, for the Uzbeks were laying siege to Balkh. However he supplied Allah-u-dín with troops and ordered his generals in the Punjab to support him. But again did the expedition of this prince fail, and he fled from Delhi in confusion to the Punjab. At the time that he entered it, a fugitive, Bábar was preparing for his fifth and last invasion of India.

[1] Dipálpúr is a town in the Montgomery district to the southwest of Lahore and forty miles from it. In Bábar's time it was a place of great importance.

Of that invasion I must be content to give the barest outline. Accompanied by his son, Humáyún, Bábar descended the Khaibar Pass to Pesháwar, halted there two days, crossed the Indus the 16th of December, and pushed on rapidly to Siálkót. On his arrival there, December 29th, he heard of the defeat and flight of Allah-u-dín[1]. Undismayed, he marched the following morning to Parsaror, midway between Siálkót and Kalánaur on the Rávi; thence to Kalánaur, where he crossed the Rávi; thence to the Biás, which he crossed, and thence to the strong fortress of Milwat, in which his former adherent Dáolát Khán, had taken refuge. Milwat soon fell. Bábar then marched through the Jálandhar Duáb to the Sutlej, placing, as he writes, 'his foot in the stirrup of resolution, and his hand on the reins of confidence-in-God,' crossed it near Rupar, then by way of Ambála, to the Jumna, opposite Sirsáwá[2]. Thence he held down the river for two marches. Two more brought him to Pánípat, fifty-three miles to the north-west of Delhi. There he halted and fortified his camp. The date was April 12, 1526.

Nine days later Ibráhím Lodí, at the head of an army computed by Bábar to have been a hundred thousand strong, attacked the invader in his intrenched camp. 'The sun had mounted spear-high,'

[1] Of this march there is a detailed and most interesting account given by Bábar in his *Memoirs*, page 290, and the pages following.
[2] Sirsáwá lies on the south bank of the Jumna, ten miles west-north-west of Sahárampur.

writes Bábar, 'when the onset of the battle began, and the combat lasted till midday, when the enemy were completely broken and routed.' The victory was in all respects decisive. Ibráhím Lodí was killed, bravely fighting, and Hindustán lay at the feet of the victor. That very day Bábar despatched troops to occupy Delhi and Agra. These results were accomplished on the 24th of April and 4th of May respectively [1].

[1] In his *Memoirs*, Bábar, after recounting how, from comparatively small beginnings, he had become conqueror 'of the noble country of Hindustán,' adds: 'This success I do not ascribe to my own strength, nor did this good fortune flow from my own efforts, but from the fountain of the favour and mercy of God.'

CHAPTER V

THE POSITION OF BÁBAR IN HINDUSTÁN

MASTER of the two great centres of power in the north-west, Bábar, with the foresight of a statesman, 'took stock' of the actual situation of Hindustán. He realised at once that he was master of Northern India, and that was all. The important provinces of Oudh, Jaunpur, and Western Behar, had revolted against Ibráhím, and though that prince had sent an army against the revolters, it seemed but too certain that the two parties would make common cause against the new invader. Then, Bengal, under its King, Nasrat Sháh; Gujarát, under Sikandar Sháh; and Málwá, under Sultán Mahmúd, were three powerful and independent kingdoms. A portion of Málwá, indeed, that represented by the fortresses, Ranthambor, at the angle formed by the confluence of the Chambal and the Banás; Sarangpur, on the Kálí Sind; Bhilsa, on the Betwá; Chanderi; and Chitor, very famous in those days, had been re-conquered by the renowned Hindu prince, Ráná Sanga. In the south of India, too, the Báhmanís had established a kingdom, and the Rájá of Vijayanagar exercised independent authority. There were, moreover, he found, a considerable number of

Ráis and Rájás who had never submitted to Muhammadan kings.

But the independence of these several princes did not, he soon recognised, constitute his greatest difficulty. That difficulty arose from the fact that the Hindu population, never conciliated by the families which had preceded his own, were hostile to the invader. 'The north of India,' writes Erskine, 'still retained much of its Hindu organisation; its system of village and district administration and government; its division into numerous little chieftainships, or petty local governments; and, in political revolutions, the people looked much more to their own immediate rulers than to the prince who governed in the capital.' In a word, never having realised the working of a well-ordered system, emanating from one all-powerful centre, they regarded the latest conqueror as an intruder whom it might be their interest to oppose.

The dread thus engendered by the arrival of a new invader, whose character and whose dispositions were alike unknown, was increased by the machinations of the Muhammadan adherents of the old families. These men argued that the success of the Mughal invader meant ruin to them. They spared no pains, then, to impress upon the Hindu population that neither their temples nor their wives and daughters would be safe from the rapine and lust of the barbarians of Central Asia. Under the influence of a terror produced by these warnings the Hindus fled from before the merciful and generous invader as he approached Agra, preferring the misery of the jungle to the apparent certainty of outrage.

To add to Bábar's troubles, there arose at this period discontent in his army. The men composing it were to a great extent mountaineers from the lofty ranges in Eastern Afghánistán. These men had followed their King with delight so long as there was a prospect of fighting. But Pánípat had given them Northern India. The march from Delhi to Agra was a march through a deserted country, at a season always hot, but the intense heat of which, in 1526, exceeded the heat of normal years. Like the Highlanders of our own Prince Charlie in '45, these highlanders murmured. They, too, longed to return to their mountain homes. The disaffection was not confined to the men. Even the chiefs complained; and their complaints became so loud that they at last reached the ears of Bábar.

Bábar had been greatly pleased with his conquest. Neither the heat nor the disaffection of the inhabitants had been able to conceal from him the fact that he had conquered the finest, the most fertile, the most valuable part of Asia. In his wonderful memoirs [1] he devotes more than twenty large printed pages to describe it. 'It is a remarkably fine country,' he begins. 'It is quite a different world compared with our countries.' He saw almost at a glance that all his work was cut out to complete the conquest in the sense he attributed to that word. Henceforth the title of King of Kábul

---

[1] Bábar's *Memoirs*, pp. 312 to 335.

was to be subjected to the higher title of Emperor of Hindustán. For him there was no turning back.

He had noted all the difficulties, and he had resolved how to meet them. A thoroughly practical man, he proceeded first to take up that which he rightly regarded as the greatest—the discontent in the army. Assembling a council of his nobles, he laid before them the actual position: told them how, after many toilsome marches and bloody fights, they had won numerous rich and extensive provinces. To abandon these and to return to Kábul would be shame indeed. 'Let not anyone who calls himself my friend,' he concluded, 'henceforward make such a proposal. But if there is any among you who cannot bring himself to stay, or to give up his purpose of returning back, let him depart.' The address produced the desired effect, and when the words were followed by action, by new encounters and by new successes, enthusiasm succeeded discontent [1].

The firmness of the conqueror was soon rewarded in a different manner. No sooner did the inhabitants, Muhammadan settlers and Hindu landowners and traders, recognise that Bábar intended his occupancy to

---

[1] To one of his friends, who found the heat unsupportable, and whom he therefore made Governor of Ghazni, Bábar, when he was firm in the saddle, sent the distich, of which the following is the translation:

'Return a hundred thanks, O Bábar, for the bounty of the merciful God
Has given you Sind, Hind, and numerous kingdoms;
If, unable to stand the heat, you long for cold,
You have only to recollect the frost and cold of Ghazni.'

be permanent, than their fears subsided. Many proofs, meanwhile, of his generous and noble nature had affected public opinion regarding him. Every day then brought accessions to his standard. Villagers and shopkeepers returned to their homes, and abundance soon reigned in camp. A little later, and the army which had been employed by Ibráhím Lodí to put down rebellion in Jaunpur and Oudh, acknowledged Bábar as their sovereign. In the interval, judiciously employing his troops, he conquered a great part of Rohilkhand; occupied the important post of Ráberí, on the Jumna; and laid siege to Itáwa and Dholpur. But troubles were preparing for him in Central India, from a quarter which it would not do for him to neglect.

These troubles were caused by Ráná Sanga, Ráná of Chitor. I have related already how this great prince —for great in every sense of the term he was—had won back from the earlier Muhammadan invaders a great portion of his hereditary dominions. He had even done more. He had defeated Ibráhím Lodí in two pitched battles, those of Bakrául and Chatáulí, and had gained from other generals sixteen in addition. Before the arrival in India of Bábar he had taken the then famous fort of Ranthambor. But he had continued, and was continuing, his career of conquest, and the news which troubled Bábar was to the effect that the great Rájpút chief had just taken the strong hill-fort of Kandar, a few miles to the eastward of Ranthambor.

Towards the end of the rainy season Bábar held a council to meet these and other difficulties. At this council it was arranged that, whilst his eldest son, Humáyún[1], then eighteen years old, should march eastward, to complete the subjection of the Duáb, Oudh, and Juánpur, Bábar should remain at Agra to superintend there the general direction of affairs. As for Ráná Sanga, it was resolved to march against him only when the enemy nearer home should have been subdued.

The expedition of Humáyún was completely successful. He conquered the country as far as the frontiers of Bihár. On his return, January 6th, 1527, Bábar subdued Biána and Dholpur, took by stratagem the fortress of Gwalior, received information of the surrender of Múltán. Then, master of the country from the Indus to the frontiers of Western Bihár, and from Kálpi and Gwalior to the Himálayas, he turned his attention to the famous Ráná of Chitor, Ráná Sanga. On February 11 he marched from Agra to encounter the army of this prince, who, joined by Muhammadan auxiliaries of the Lodí party, had advanced too, and had encamped at Bisáwar, some

---

[1] In the famous *Memoirs*, pp. 302-3, is to be found the following note, inserted by Humáyún: 'At this same station,' the station of Sháhábád, on the left bank of the Sarsutí, reached on the march to Pánípat, 'and this same day,' March 6, 1526, 'the razor or scissors were first applied to Humáyún's beard. As my honoured father mentioned in these commentaries the time of his first using the razor, in humble emulation of him I have commemorated the same circumstance regarding myself. I was then eighteen years of age. Now that I am forty-six, I, Muhammad Humáyún, am transcribing a copy of these *Memoirs* from the copy in his late Majesty's own handwriting.'

twelve miles from Biána and some sixty-two, by that place, from Agra. Bábar advanced to Síkrí, now Fatehpur-Síkrí, and halted. In some skirmishes which followed the Rájpúts had all the advantage, and a great discouragement fell on the soldiers of Bábar. He contented himself for the moment with making his camp as defensible as possible, and by sending a party to ravage Mewát.

Cooped up in camp, discouraged by the aspect of affairs, Bábar, uneasy at the forced inaction, passed in review the events of his life, and recognised with humility and penitence that throughout it he had habitually violated one of the strictest injunctions of the Kurán, that which forbids the drinking of wine. He resolved at once to amend. Sending then for his golden wine-cups and his silver goblets he had them destroyed in his presence, and gave the proceeds of the sale of the precious metal to the poor. All the wine in the camp was rendered undrinkable or poured on the ground. Three hundred of his nobles followed his example.

Sensible at length that the situation could not be prolonged, Bábar, on March 12th, advanced two miles towards the enemy, halted, and again advanced the day following to a position he had selected as favourable to an engagement. Here he ranged his troops in order of battle. On the 16th the Rájpúts and their allies advanced, and the battle joined. Of it Bábar has written in his memoirs a picturesque and, doubtless, a faithful account. It must suffice here to say that he gained a victory so decisive[1], that on the morrow of it Rájpútána lay at his feet. He at once pushed on to Biána, thence into Mewát, and reduced the entire province to obedience. But the effects of his victory were not limited to conquests achieved by himself. Towns in the Duáb which had revolted, returned to their allegiance or were recovered. When the Duáb had been completely pacified Bábar turned his arms, first, against the Hindu chiefs of Central India, the leader of whom was at the time the Rájá of Chandérí. He had reached the town and fortress of that name when information came to him that his generals in the east had been unfortunate, and had been compelled to fall back from Lucknow upon Kanauj. Unshaken by this intelligence, the importance of which he admitted, he persevered in the siege of Chandérí, and in a few days stormed the fortress. Having secured the submission of the country he marched rapidly eastward, joined his defeated generals near Kanauj, threw a bridge across the Ganges near that place, drove the enemy—the remnant of the Lodí party—before him, re-occupied Lucknow, crossed the Gúmtí and the Gogra, and forced the dispirited foe to disperse. He then returned to Agra to resume the threads of the administration he was arranging.

But he was not allowed time to remain quiet. The

[1] Ráná Sanga was severely wounded, and the choicest chieftains of his army were slain. The Ráná died the same year at Baswa on the frontiers of Mewát.

old Muhammadan party in Jaunpur had never been effectively subdued. The rich kingdom of Behar, adjoining that of Jaunpur, had, up to this time, been unassailed. And now the Muhammadan nobles of both districts combined to place in the hands of a prince of the house of Lodí—the same who had aided Sanga Ráná against Bábar—the chief authority in the united kingdom. The conspiracy had been conducted with so much secrecy that the result of it only reached Bábar on the 1st of February, 1529. He was then at Dholpur, a place which he greatly affected, engaged with his nobles in laying out gardens, and otherwise improving and beautifying the place. That very day he returned to Agra, and taking with him such troops as he had at hand, marched the day following to join his son Askarí's army, then at Dakdakí, a village near Karra [1], on the right bank of the Ganges. He reached that place on the 27th, and found Askarí's army on the opposite bank of the river. He at once directed that prince to conform his movements on the left bank to those of his own on the right.

The news which reached Bábar here was not of a nature to console. The enemy, to the number of a hundred thousand, had rallied round the standard of Máhmud Lodí; whilst one of his own generals, Sher Khán, whom he had distinguished by marks of his favour, had joined the insurgents and had

---

[1] Karra is now in ruins. It is in the tahsil or district of the same name in the Allahabad division. In the times of Bábar and Akbar it was very prosperous.

occupied Benares with his division. Máhmud Lodí was besieging Chanar, twenty-six miles from the sacred city.

Bábar immediately advanced, compelled Máhmud Lodí to raise the siege of Chanar, forced Sher Khán to evacuate Benares and re-cross the Ganges, and, crossing the Karamnása, encamped beyond Chausá, at the confluence of that river and the Ganges, and Baksar. Marching thence, he drove his enemy before him until he reached Arrah. There he assumed the sovereignty of Behar, and there he learned that Máhmud Lodí, attended by but a few followers, had taken refuge with the King of Bengal.

Nasrat Sháh, King of Bengal, had married a niece of Máhmud Lodí. He had entered into a kind of convention with Bábar that neither prince was to invade the territories of the other, but, despite this convention, he had occupied the province of Sáran or Chaprá, and had taken up with his army a position near the junction of the Gogra with the Ganges, very strong for defensive purposes. Bábar resolved to compel the Bengal army to abandon that position. There was, he soon found, but one way to accomplish that end, and that was by the use of force. Ranging then his army in six divisions, he directed that four, under his son Askarí, then on the left bank of the Ganges, should cross the Gogra, march upon the enemy, and attempt to draw them from their camp, and follow them up the Gogra; whilst the two others, under his own personal direction, should cross the Ganges, then the Gogra, and attack the enemy's camp, cutting him off from his base. The combination, carried out on the 6th of May, entirely succeeded. The Bengal army was completely defeated, and the victory was, in every sense of the word, decisive. Peace was concluded with Bengal on the conditions that the province, now known as Western Behar, should be ceded to Bábar; that neither prince should support the enemies of the other, and that neither should molest the dominions of the other.

Thus far I have been guided mainly by the memoirs of the illustrious man whose achievements I have briefly recorded. There is but little more to tell. Shortly after his return from his victorious campaign in Behar his health began to decline. The fact could not be concealed, and an account of it reached his eldest son, Humáyún, then Governor of Badakshán. That prince, making over his government to his brother, Hindal, hastened to Agra. He arrived there early in 1530, was most affectionately received, and by his sprightly wit and genial manners, made many friends. He had been there but six months when he was attacked by a serious illness. When the illness was at its height, and the life of the young prince was despaired of, an incident occurred which shows, in a manner not to be mistaken, the unselfishness and affection of Bábar. It is thus related in the supplemental chapter to the *Memoirs*[1].

---

[1] This chapter was added by the translators. The same circumstance is related also by Mr. Erskine in his *Bábar and Humáyún*.

'When all hopes from medicine were over, and whilst several men of skill were talking to the Emperor of the melancholy situation of his son, Abul Báká, a personage highly venerated for his knowledge and piety, remarked to Bábar that in such a case the Almighty had sometimes vouchsafed to receive the most valuable thing possessed by one friend, as an offering in exchange for the life of another. Bábar exclaimed that, of all things, his life was dearest to Humáyún, as Humáyún's was to him; that his life, therefore, he most cheerfully devoted as a sacrifice for that of his son; and prayed the Most High to vouchsafe to accept it.' Vainly did his courtiers remonstrate. He persisted, we are told, in his resolution; walked thrice round the dying prince, a solemnity similar to that used by the Muhammadans in sacrifices, and, retiring, prayed earnestly. After a time he was heard to exclaim: 'I have borne it away! I have borne it away!' The Musalmán historians relate that almost from that moment Humáyún began to recover and the strength of Bábar began proportionately to decay. He lingered on to the end of the year 1530. On the 26th December he restored his soul to his Maker, in his palace of the Chárbágh, near Agra, in the forty-ninth year of his age. His remains were, in accordance with his dying request, conveyed to Kábul, where they were interred in a lovely spot, about a mile from the city.

Amongst the famous conquerors of the world Bábar will always occupy a very high place. His character created his career. Inheriting but the shadow of a small kingdom in Central Asia, he died master of the territories lying between the Karamnásá and the Oxus, and those between the Narbadá and the Himálayas. His nature was a joyous nature. Generous, confiding, always hopeful, he managed to attract the affection of all with whom he came in contact. He was keenly sensitive to all that was beautiful in nature; had cultivated his own remarkable talents to a degree quite unusual in the age in which he lived; and was gifted with strong affections and a very vivid imagination. He loved war and glory, but he did not neglect the arts of peace. He made it a duty to inquire into the condition of the races whom he subdued and to devise for them ameliorating measures. He was fond of gardening, of architecture, of music, and he was no mean poet. But the greatest glory of his character was that attributed to him by one who knew him well, and who thus recorded his opinion in Taríkhí Reshídí. 'Of all his qualities,' wrote Haidar Mirzá, 'his generosity and humanity took the lead.' Though he lived long enough only to conquer and not long enough to consolidate, the task of conquering could hardly have been committed to hands more pure.

Bábar left four sons: Muhammad Humáyún Mirzá, who succeeded him, born April 5, 1508: Kámrán Mirzá, Hindal Mirzá, and Askarí Mirzá. Before his death he had introduced Humáyún to a specially convened council of ministers as his successor, and had given him his dying injunctions. The points upon which he had specially laid stress were: the conscientious discharge of duties to God and man; the honest and assiduous administration of justice; the seasoning of punishment to the guilty with the extension of tenderness and mercy to the ignorant and penitent, with protection to the poor and defenceless; he besought Humáyún, moreover, to deal kindly and affectionately towards his brothers.

Thus died, in the flower of his manhood, the illustrious chief who introduced the Mughal dynasty into India; who, conquering the provinces of the North-west and some districts in the centre of the peninsula, acquired for that dynasty the prescriptive right to claim them as its own. He had many great qualities. But, in Hindustán, he had had neither the time nor the opportunity to introduce into the provinces he had conquered such a system of administration as would weld the parts theretofore separate into one homogeneous whole. It may be doubted whether, great as he was, he possessed to a high degree the genius of constructive legislation. Nowhere had he given any signs of it. In Kábul and in Hindustán alike, he had pursued the policy of the conquerors who had preceded him, that of bestowing conquered provinces and districts on adherents, to be governed by them in direct responsibility to himself, each according to his own plan. Thus it happened that when he died the provinces in India which acknowledged him as master were bound together by that tie alone. Agra had nothing in common with Lucknow; Delhi with Jaunpur. Heavy tolls marked the divisions of territories, inhabited by races of different origin, who were only bound together by the sovereignty of Bábar over all. He bequeathed to his son, Humáyún, then, a congeries of territories uncemented by any bond of union or of common interest, except that which had been embodied in his life. In a word, when he died, the Mughal dynasty, like the Muhammadan dynasties which had preceded it, had shot down no roots into the soil of Hindustán.

CHAPTER VI

HUMÁYÚN AND THE EARLY DAYS OF AKBAR

BRAVE, genial, witty, a charming companion, highly educated, generous, and merciful, Humáyún was even less qualified than his father to found a dynasty on principles which should endure. Allied to his many virtues were many compromising defects. He was volatile, thoughtless, and unsteady. He was swayed by no strong sense of duty. His generosity was apt to degenerate into prodigality; his attachments into weakness. He was unable to concentrate his energies for a time in any serious direction, whilst for comprehensive legislation he had neither the genius nor the inclination. He was thus eminently unfitted to consolidate the conquest his father had bequeathed to him.

It is unnecessary to relate in detail a history of the eight years which followed his accession. So unskilful was his management, and so little did he acquire the confidence and esteem of the races under his sway, that when, in April, 1540, he was defeated at Kanauj, by Sher Khán Sur, a nobleman who had submitted to Bábar, but who had risen against his son—whom he succeeded under the title of Sher Sháh—the entire edifice crumbled in his hand. After some adventures, Humáyún found himself, January, 1541, a fugitive with a mere handful of followers, at Rohri opposite the island of Bukkur on the Indus, in Sind. He had lost the inheritance bequeathed him by his father.

Humáyún spent altogether two and a half years in Sind, engaged in a vain attempt to establish himself in that province. The most memorable event of his sojourn there was the birth, on the 15th of October, 1542, of a son, called by him Jalál-ud-dín Muhammad Akbar. I propose to relate now the incidents which led to a result so important in the history of India.

In 1541, Humáyún, whose troops were engaged in besieging Bukkur, distrusting the designs of his brother Hindal, whom he had commissioned to attack and occupy the rich province of Schwán, appointed a meeting with the latter at the town of Pátar, some twenty miles to the west of the Indus. There he found Hindal, surrounded by his nobles, prepared to receive him right royally. During the festivities which followed, the mother of Hindal—who, it may be remarked, was not the mother of Humáyún—gave a grand entertainment, to which she invited all the ladies of the court. Amongst these Humáyún especially noted a girl called Hámidá, the daughter of a nobleman who had been preceptor to Hindal. So struck was he that he inquired on the spot whether the girl were betrothed. He was told in reply that, although she had been promised, no ceremony of betrothal had as yet taken place. 'In that case,' said Humáyún, 'I will marry her.' Hindal protested against the suddenly formed resolution, and threatened, if it were persisted in, to quit his brother's service. A quarrel, which had almost ended in a rupture, then ensued between the brothers. But the pleadings of Hindal's mother, who favoured the match, brought Hindal to acquiescence, and, the next day, Hámidá, who had just completed her fourteenth year, was married to Humáyún. A few days later, the happy pair repaired to the camp before Bukkur.

The times, however, were unfavourable to the schemes of Humáyún. All his plans miscarried, and, in the spring of 1542, he and his young wife had to flee for safety to the barren deserts of Marwar. In August they reached Jaisalmer, but, repulsed by its Rájá, they had to cross the great desert, suffering terribly during the journey from want of water. Struggling bravely, however, they reached, on August 22nd, the fort of Amarkót, on the edge of the desert. The Ráná of the fort received them hospitably, and there, on Sunday October the 15th, Hámidá Begam gave birth to Akbar. Humáyún had quitted Amarkót four days previously, to invade the district of Jun. His words, when the news was brought to him, deserve to be recorded. 'As soon,' wrote one who attended him, 'as the Emperor had finished his thanksgivings to God, the Amírs were introduced, and offered their congratulations. He then called Jouher (the historian, author of the Tezkereh al

Vakiat) and asked what he had committed to his charge. Jouher answered: "Two hundred Sháhrukhís" (Khorásání gold coins), a silver wristlet and a musk-bag; adding, that the two former had been returned to their owners. On this Humáyún ordered the musk-bag to be brought, and, having broken it on a china plate, he called his nobles, and divided it among them, as the royal present in honour of his son's birth.' ... 'This event,' adds Jouher, 'diffused its fragrance over the whole habitable world.'

The birth of the son brought no immediate good fortune to the father. In July, 1543, Humáyún was compelled to quit Sind, and, accompanied by his wife and son and a small following, set out with the intention of reaching Kandahár. He had arrived at Shál, when he learnt that his brother, Askarí, with a considerable force, was close at hand, and that immediate flight was necessary. He and his wife were ready, but what were they to do with the child, then only a year old, quite unfit to make a rapid journey on horseback, in the boisterous weather then prevailing? Reckoning, not without reason, that the uncle would not make war against a baby, they decided to leave him, with the whole of their camp-equipage and baggage, and the ladies who attended him. They then set out, and riding hard, reached the Persian frontier in safety. Scarcely had they gone when Askarí Mirzá arrived. Veiling his disappointment at the escape of his brother with some soft words, he treated the young prince with affection, had him conveyed to Kandahár, of which place he was Governor, and placed there under the supreme charge of his own wife, the ladies who had been his nurses still remaining in attendance.

In this careful custody the young prince remained during the whole of the year 1544. But soon after the dawn of the following year a change in his condition occurred. His father, with the aid of troops supplied him by Sháh Tahmásp, invaded Western Afghánistán, making straight across the desert for Kandahár. Alarmed at this movement, and dreading lest Humáyún should recover his child, Kámrán sent peremptory orders that the boy should be transferred to Kábul. When the confidential officers whom Kámrán had instructed on this subject reached Kandahár, the ministers of Askarí Mirzá held a council to consider whether or not the demand should be complied with. Some, believing the star of Humáyún to be in the ascendant, advised that the boy should be sent, under honourable escort, to his father. Others maintained that Prince Askarí had acted so treacherously towards his eldest brother that no act of penitence would now avail, and that it was better to continue to deserve the favour of Kámrán. The arguments of the latter prevailed, and though the winter was unusually severe, the infant prince and his sister, Bakhshí Bánu Begam, were despatched with their attendants to Kábul. After some adventures, which made the escort apprehend an attempt at rescue, the party reached Kábul in safety, and there Kámrán confided his nephew to the care of his great-aunt, Khánzáda Begam, the whilom favourite sister of the Emperor Bábar. This illustrious lady maintained in their duties the nurses and attendants who had watched over the early days of the young prince, and during the short time of her superintendence she bestowed upon him the tenderest care. Unhappily that superintendence lasted only a few months. The capture of Kandahár by Humáyún in the month of September following (1545) threw Kámrán into a state of great perplexity. A suspicious and jealous man, and regarding the possession of Akbar as a talisman he could use against Humáyún, he removed the boy from the care of his grand-aunt, and confided him to a trusted adherent, Kuch Kilán by name. But events marched very quickly in those days. Humáyún, having established a firm base at Kandahár, set out with an army for Kábul, appeared before that city the first week in November, and compelled it to surrender to him on the 15th. Kámrán had escaped to Ghazní: but the happy father had the gratification of finding the son from whom he had been so long separated. The boy's mother, Hámidá Begam, did not arrive till the spring of the following year, but, meanwhile, Kuch Kilán was removed, and the prince's former governor, known as Atká Khán[1], was restored to his post.

[1] His real name was Shams-ud-dín Muhammad of Ghazní. He

For the moment splendour and prosperity surrounded the boy. But when winter came, Humáyún, who meanwhile had recovered Badakshán, resolved to pass the coldest months of the year at Kílá Zafar, in that province. But on his way thither he was seized with an illness so dangerous that his life was despaired of. He recovered indeed after two months' strict confinement to his bed, but, in the interval, many of his nobles, believing his end was assured, had repaired to the courts of his brothers, and Kámrán, aided by troops supplied by his father-in-law, had regained Kábul, and, with Kábul, possession of the person of Akbar. One of the first acts of the conqueror was to remove Atká Khán from the person of the prince, and to replace him by one of his own servants.

But Humáyún had no sooner regained his strength than he marched to recover his capital. Defeating, in the suburbs, a detachment of the best troops of Kámrán, he established his head-quarters on the Koh-Akabain which commands the town, and commenced to cannonade it. The fire after some days became so severe and caused so much damage that, to stop it, Kámrán sent to his brother to declare that unless the fire should cease, he would expose the young Akbar on the walls at the point where it was hottest[1].

had saved the life of Humáyún in 1540, at the battle of Kanauj, fought against Sher Sháh.

[1] Abulfazl relates in the Akbarnáná that the prince actually was exposed, and Haidar Mirzá, Badauní, Ferishtá, and others follow him; but Bayazid, who was present, though he minutely describes other atrocities in his memoirs, does not mention this; whilst Jouher,

Humáyún ordered the firing to cease. He continued the siege, however, and on the 28th of April (1547) entered the city a conqueror. Kámrán had escaped the previous night.

Kámrán had fled to Badakshán. Thither Humáyún followed him. But, in the winter that followed, some of his most powerful nobles revolted, and deserted to Kámrán. Humáyún, after some marches and countermarches, determined in the summer of 1548 to make a decisive effort to settle his northern dominions. He marched, then, in June from Kábul, taking with him Akbar and Akbar's mother. On reaching Gulbahan he sent back to Kábul Akbar and his mother, and marching on Talikán, forced Kámrán to surrender. Having settled his northern territories the Emperor, as he was still styled, returned to Kábul.

He quitted it again, in the late spring of 1549, to attempt Balkh, in the western Kunduz territory. The Uzbeks, however, repulsed him, and he returned to Kábul for the winter of 1550. Then ensued a very curious scene. Kámrán, whose failure to join Humáyún in the expedition against Balkh had been the main cause of his retreat, and who had subsequently gone into open rebellion, had, after Humáyún's defeat, made a disastrous campaign on the Oxus, and had sent his submission to Humáyún. That prince, consigning the government of Kábul to Akbar, then

in his private memoirs of Humáyún, a translation of which by Major Charles Stewart appeared in 1832, states the story as I have given it in the text.

eight years old, with Muhammad Kásim Khán Birlás as his tutor, marched from the capital to gain possession of the person of his brother. So careless, however, were his movements that Kámrán, who had planned the manœuvre, surprised him at the upper end of the defile of Kipchak, and forced him to take refuge in flight. During the flight Humáyún was badly wounded, but nevertheless managed to reach the top of the Sirtan Pass in safety. There he was in comparative security. Meanwhile Kámrán had marched upon and captured Kábul, and, for the third time, Akbar found himself a prisoner in the hands of his uncle. Humáyún did not submit tamely to this loss. Rallying his adherents, he recrossed the mountains, and marched on the city. Arriving at Shutargardan he saw the army of Kámrán drawn up to oppose him. After some days of fruitless negotiation for a compromise Humáyún ordered the attack. It resulted in a complete victory and the flight of Kámrán. For a moment Humáyún feared lest Kámrán should have carried his son with him in his flight. But, before he could enter the city, he was intensely relieved by the arrival in camp of Akbar, accompanied by Hásán Akhtá, to whose care he had been entrusted. The next day he entered the city.

This time the conquest was decisive and lasting. In the distribution of awards which followed Humáyún did not omit his son. He bestowed upon Akbar as a jaghír the district of Chirkh, and nominated Hájí Muhammad Khán of Sístán as his minister.

with the care of his education. During the year that followed the causes of the troubles of Humáyún disappeared one by one. Kámrán indeed once more appeared in arms, but only to be hunted down so vigorously that he was forced to surrender (August, 1553). He was exiled to Mekka, where he died four years later. Hindal Mirzá, another brother, had been slain some eighteen months before, during the pursuit of Kámrán. Askarí Mirzá, the other brother, in whose nature treachery seemed ingrained, had been exiled to Mekka in 1551[1], and though he still survived he was harmless. Relieved thus of his brothers, Humáyún contemplated the conquest of Kashmír, but his nobles and their followers were so averse to the expedition that he was forced, unwillingly, to renounce it. He consoled himself by crossing the Indus. Whilst encamped in the districts between that river and the Jehlam he ordered the repair, tantamount to a reconstruction on an enlarged plan, of the fort at Pesháwar. He was contemplating even then the invasion of India, and he was particularly anxious that he should possess a *point d'appui* beyond the passes on which his army could concentrate. He pushed the works so vigorously that the fort was ready by the end of the year (1554). He then returned to Kábul. During the winter and early spring that followed, there came to a head in Hindustán the crisis which gave him the opportunity of carrying his plans into effect.

[1] He died there in 1558.

CHAPTER VII

Humáyún invades India. His Death

SHER KHÁN SUR, who had defeated Humáyún at Kanauj in 1540, had used his victory to possess himself of the territories which Bábar had conquered, and to add somewhat to them. He was an able man, but neither did he, more than the prince whom he supplanted, possess the genius of consolidation and union. He governed on the system of detached camps, each province and district being separately administered. He died in 1545 from injuries received at the siege of Kálinjar, just as that strong fort surrendered to his arms.

His second son, Salim Sháh Sur, known also as Sultán Islám, succeeded him, and reigned for between seven and eight years. He must have been dimly conscious of the weakness of the system he had inherited, for the greater part of his reign was spent in combating the intrigues of the noblemen who held the several provinces under him. On his death, leaving a child of tender years to succeed him, the nobles took the upper hand. The immediate result was the murder of the young prince, after a nominal rule of three days, and the seizure of the throne by his maternal uncle, who proclaimed himself as Sultán under the title of Muhammad Sháh Adel. He was ignorant, cruel, unprincipled, and a sensualist of a very pronounced type. He had, however, the good fortune to attach to his throne a Hindu, named Hemu, who, originally a shopkeeper of Rewárí, a town of Mewát, showed talents so considerable, that he was eventually allowed to concentrate in his own hands all the power of the State. The abilities of Hemu did not, however, prevent the break-up of the territories which Sher Sháh had bequeathed to his son. Ibráhím Khán revolted at Biáná, and occupying Agra and Delhi, proclaimed himself Sultán. Ahmad Khán, Governor of the country north-west of the Sutlej, seized the Punjab, and proclaimed himself king under the title of Sikandar Sháh. Shujá Khán seized the kingdom of Málwá, whilst two rival claimants disputed the eastern provinces. In the contests which followed Sikandar Sháh for the moment obtained the upper hand. He defeated Ibráhím Khán at Farah, twenty miles from Agra, then marched on and occupied Delhi. He was preparing to head an expedition to recover Jaunpur and Behar, when he heard of danger threatening him from Kábul.

The events that followed were important only in their results. Humáyún marched from Kábul for the Indus in November, 1554, at the head of a small army, which, however, gathered strength as he advanced. Akbar accompanied him. Crossing the Indus the 2nd of January, 1555, Humáyún made for

Ráwal Pindí, then pushed on for Kálánaur, on the further side of the Ráví. There he divided his forces, sending his best general, Bairám Khán, into Jálandhar, whilst he marched on Lahore, and despatched thence his special favourite, Abdul Má'alí, to occupy Dípálpur, then an important centre, commanding the country between the capital and Múltán.

Events developed themselves very rapidly. Bairám Khán defeated the generals of Sikandar Sháh at Machhíwára on the Sutlej, and then marched on the town of Sirhind. Sikandar, hoping to crush him there, hurried to that place with a vastly superior force. Bairám intrenched himself, and wrote to Humáyún for aid. Humáyún despatched the young Akbar, and followed a few days later. Before they could come, Sikandar had arrived but had hesitated to attack. The hesitation lost him. As soon as Humáyún arrived, he precipitated a general engagement. The victory was decisive. Sikandar Sháh fled to the Siwáliks, and Humáyún, with his victorious army, marched on Delhi. Occupying it the 23rd of July, he despatched one division of it to overrun Rohilkhand, another to occupy Agra. He had previously sent Abdul Má'alí to secure the Punjab.

But his troubles were not yet over. Hemu, the general and chief minister of Muhammad Sháh Adel, had defeated the pretender to the throne of Bengal, who had invaded the North-west Provinces, near Kálpi on the Jumna, and that capable leader was preparing to march on Delhi. Sikandar Sháh, too, who had been defeated at Sirhind, was beginning to show signs of life in the Punjab. In the face of these difficulties Humáyún decided to remain at Delhi himself, whilst he despatched Akbar with Bairám Khán as his 'Atálik,' or adviser, to settle matters in the Punjab.

We must first follow Akbar. That prince reached Sirhind early in January, 1556. Joined there by many of the nobles whom Abdul Má'alí, the favourite of his father, had disgusted by his haughtiness, he crossed the Sutlej at Phillaur, marched on Sultánpur in the Kángra district, and thence, in pursuit of Sikandar Sháh, to Hariána. The morning of his arrival there, information reached him of a serious accident which had happened to Humáyún. He at once suspended the forward movement, and marched on Kálánaur, there to await further intelligence. As he approached that place, a despatch was placed in his hands, drafted by order of Humáyún, giving hopes of speedy recovery. But, a little later, another courier arrived, bearing the news of the Emperor's death. Akbar was at once proclaimed.

The situation was a trying one for a boy who had lived but thirteen years and four months. He occupied, indeed, the Punjab. His servants held Sirhind, Delhi, and possibly Agra. But he was aware that Hemu, flushed with two victories, for he had obtained a second over another pretender, was marching towards the last-named city with an army of fifty thousand men and five hundred elephants, with the avowed intention of restoring the rule of Muhammad

Sháh Adel. To add to his difficulties he heard a few days later that the viceroy placed by his father at Kábul had revolted.

Humáyún had met his death by a fall from the top of the staircase leading to the terraced roof of his library in the palace of Delhi. He lingered four days, the greater part of the time in a state of insensibility, and expired the evening of the 24th of January, in the forty-eighth year of his age. Tardí Beg Khán, the most eminent of all the nobles at the capital, and actually Governor of the city, assumed on the spot the general direction of affairs. His first care was to conceal the incident from the public until he could arrange to make the succession secure for the young Akbar, to whom he sent expresses conveying details. By an ingenious stratagem he managed to conceal the death of the Emperor for seventeen days. Then, on the 10th of February, he repaired with the nobles to the great Mosque, and caused the prayer for the Emperor to be recited in the name of Akbar. His next act was to despatch the insignia of the empire with the Crown jewels, accompanied by the officers of the household, the Imperial Guards, and a possible rival to the throne in the person of a son of Humáyún's brother, Kámrán, to the head-quarters of the new Emperor in the Punjab. He then proceeded to take measures to secure the capital against the threatened attack of Hemu.

CHAPTER VIII

Akbar's Fight for his Father's Throne

THE news of his father's death, I have said, reached Akbar as he was entering the town of Kálánaur at the head of his army. At the moment he had not heard of the revolt at Kábul, nor had his adviser, Bairám Khán, dwelt in his mind on the probability of a movement by Hemu against Delhi. In the first few days, then, it seemed as though there were but one enemy in the field, and that enemy the Sikandar Sháh, to suppress whom his father had sent him to the Punjab. That prince was still in arms, slowly retreating in the direction of Kashmír. It appeared, then, to the young Emperor and his adviser that their first business should be to secure the Punjab; that to effect that object they must follow up Sikandar Sháh. The army accordingly broke up from Kálánaur, pushed after Sikandar, and drove him to take refuge in the fort of Mánkót, in the lower ranges of the Siwáliks. As Mánkót was very strong, and tidings of untoward events alike in Hindustán and Kábul reached them, the leaders contented themselves with leaving a force to blockade that fortress, and returned to Jálandhar.

It was time indeed. Not only had Kábul revolted, but Hemu, his army increasing with every step, had taken Agra without striking a blow, and was pursuing the retreating garrison towards Delhi. A day later came the information that he had defeated the Mughal army close to Delhi, and had occupied that capital. Tardí Beg, with the remnants of the defeated force, had fled towards Sirhind.

In the multitude of counsellors there is not always wisdom. When Akbar heard of the success of Hemu, he assembled his warrior-nobles and asked their advice. With one exception they all urged him to fall back on Kábul. That he could recover his mountain-capital they felt certain, and there he could remain until events should be propitious for a fresh invasion of India. Against this recommendation Bairám Khán raised his powerful voice. He urged a prompt march across the Sutlej, a junction with Tardí Beg in Sirhind, and an immediate attempt thence against Hemu. Delhi, he said, twice gained and twice lost, must at all hazards be won back. Delhi was the decisive point, not Kábul. Master of the former, one could easily recover the latter. The instincts of Akbar coincided with the advice of his Atálik, and an immediate march across the Sutlej was directed.

Akbar and Bairám saw in fact that their choice lay between empire in Hindustán and a small kingdom in Kábul. For they knew from their adherents in

India that Hemu was preparing to supplement the occupation of Delhi by the conquest of the Punjab. To be beforehand with him, to transfer the initiative to themselves, always a great matter with Asiatics, was almost a necessity to secure success. Akbar marched then from Jálandhar in October, and crossing the Sutlej, gained the town of Sirhind. There he was joined by Tardí Beg and the nobles who had been defeated by Hemu under the walls of Delhi. The circumstances which followed their arrival sowed in the heart of Akbar the first seeds of revolt against the licence of power assumed by his Atálik. Tardí Beg was a Turkí nobleman, who, in the contest between Humáyún and his brothers, had more than once shifted his allegiance, but he had finally enrolled himself as a partisan of the father of Akbar. When Humáyún died, it was Tardí Beg who by his tact and loyalty succeeded in arranging for the bloodless succession of Akbar, though a son of Kámrán was in Delhi at the time. After his defeat by Hemu, he had, it is true, in the opinion of some of the other nobles, too hastily evacuated Delhi; but an error in tactics is not a crime, and he had at least brought a powerful reinforcement to Akbar in Sirhind. But there had ever been jealousy between Bairám Khán and Tardí Beg. This jealousy was increased in the heart of Bairám by religious differences, for Bairám belonged to the Shí'áh division of the Muhammadan creed, and Tardí Beg was a Sunní. On the arrival of the latter at Sirhind, then, Bairám summoned him to his tent and had him assassinated[1]. Akbar was greatly displeased at this act of violence, and Bairám did not succeed in justifying himself. It may be inferred that he excused himself on the ground that such an act was necessary, in the interests of discipline, to secure the proper subordination of the nobles.

Meanwhile Hemu remained at Delhi, amusing himself with the new title of Rájá which he had assumed, and engaged in collecting troops. When, however, he heard that Akbar had reached Sirhind, he despatched his artillery to Pánípat, fifty-three miles to the north of Delhi, intending to follow himself with the infantry and cavalry. But, on his side, Akbar was moving from Sirhind towards the same place. More than that, he had taken the precaution to despatch in advance a force of ten thousand horsemen, under the command of Álí Kulí Khán-í-Shaibání, the general who had fought with Tardí Beg against Hemu at Delhi, and who had condemned his too hasty retirement[2]. Álí Kulí rode as far as Pánípat, and noting there the guns of Hemu's army, unsupported, he dashed upon them and captured them all.

[1] Vide Dowson's Sir Henry Elliot's *History of India as told by its own Historians*, vol. v. page 251 and note. The only historian who states that Akbar gave a 'kind of permission' to this atrocious deed is Badauní. He is practically contradicted by Abulfazl and Ferishtá. In Blochmann's admirable edition of the *Ain-i-Akbari*, p. 315, the story is repeated as told by Badauní, but the translator adds the words: 'Akbar was displeased. Bairám's hasty act was one of the chief causes of the distrust with which the Chagataí nobles looked upon him.'

[2] Blochmann's *Ain-i-Akbari*, p. 319.

For this brilliant feat of arms he was created a Khán Zamán, by which he is henceforth known in history. This misfortune greatly depressed Hemu, for, it is recorded, the guns had been obtained from Turkey, and were regarded with great reverence. However, without further delay, he pressed on to Pánípat.

Akbar and Bairám were marching on to the plains of Pánípat on the morning of the 5th of November, 1556, when they sighted the army of Hemu moving towards them. The thought must, I should think, have been present in the mind of the young prince that just thirty years before his grandfather, Bábar, had, on the same plain, struck down the house of Lodí, and won the empire of Hindustán. He was confronted now by the army of the usurper, connected by marriage with that House of Sur which had expelled his own father. The battle, he knew, would be the decisive battle of the century. But, prescient as he was, he could not foresee that it would prove the starting-point for the establishment in India of a dynasty which would last for more than two hundred years, and would then require another invasion from the north, and another battle of Pánípat to strike it down; the advent of another race of foreigners from an island in the Atlantic to efface it.

Hemu had divided his army into three divisions. In front marched the five hundred elephants, each bestridden by an officer of rank, and led by Hemu, on his own favourite animal, in person. He dashed first against the advancing left wing of the Mughals and threw it into disorder, but as his lieutenants failed to support the attack with infantry, he drew off, and threw himself on the centre, commanded by Bairám in person. That astute general had directed his archers, in anticipation of such an attack, to direct their arrows at the faces of the riders. One of these arrows pierced the eye of Hemu, who fell back in his howdah, for the moment insensible. The fall of their leader spread consternation among the followers. The attack slackened, then ceased. The soldiers of Bairám soon converted the cessation into a rout. The elephant on which Hemu rode, without a driver—for the driver had been killed [1]—made off instinctively towards the jungle. A nobleman, a follower and distant relative of Bairám, Sháh Kulí Mahrám-i-Bahárlu, followed the elephant, not knowing who it was who rode it. Coming up with it and catching hold of the rope on its neck, he discovered that it was the wounded Hemu who had become his captive [2]. He led him to Bairám. Bairám took him to the youthful prince, who throughout the day had shown courage and conduct, but who had left the ordering of the battle to his Atálik. The scene that followed is thus told by contemporary writers. Bairám said to his master, as he presented to him the wounded general: 'This is your first war: prove your sword on this infidel, for it will be a meritorious deed.'

[1] This is the generally received story, though Abulfazl states that the driver, to save his own life, betrayed his master. Elliot, vol. v. p. 253, note.

[2] Compare Elliot, vol. v. p. 253, and Blochmann's *Ain-i-Akbari*, p. 359.

Akbar replied : 'He is now no better than a dead man; how can I strike him ? If he had sense and strength I would try my sword (that is I would fight him).' On Akbar's refusal, Bairám himself cut down the prisoner.

Bairám sent his cavalry to pursue the enemy to Delhi, giving them no respite, and the next day, marching the fifty-three miles without a halt, the Mughal army entered the city. Thenceforward Akbar was without a formidable rival in India. He occupied the position his grandfather had occupied thirty years before. It remained to be seen whether the boy would use the opportunity which his father and grandfather had alike failed to grasp. To show the exact nature of the task awaiting him, I propose to devote the next chapter to a brief survey of the condition of India at the time of his accession, and in that following to inquire how the boy of fourteen was likely to benefit by the tutelage of Bairám Khán.

CHAPTER IX

GENERAL CONDITION OF INDIA IN THE MIDDLE OF THE SIXTEENTH CENTURY

THE empire conquered south of the Sutlej by the Afghán predecessors of the Mughal had no claim to be regarded as the empire of Hindustán. It was rather the empire of Delhi, that is, of the provinces called up to the year 1857 the North-western Provinces, including that part of the Bengal Presidency which we know as Western Behar, and some districts in the Central Provinces and Rájpútána. It included, likewise, the Punjab. For a moment, indeed, the princes of the House of Tughlak could claim supremacy over Bengal and almost the whole of Southern India, but the first invasion from the north gave the opportunity which the Hindu princes of the south seized to shake off the uncongenial yoke, and it had not been re-imposed. The important kingdom of Orissa, extending from the mouth of the Ganges to that of the Godávarí, had always maintained its independence. Western India, too, had for some time ceased to acknowledge the sway of the foreign invader, and its several states had become kingdoms.

Thus, at the accession of Akbar, the westernmost portion of India, the kingdom of Gujarát, ruled over by a Muhammadan prince of Afghán blood, was independent. It had been overrun, indeed, by Humáyún, but on his flight from India it had re-asserted itself, and had not since been molested. Indeed it had carried on a not unsuccessful war with its nearest neighbour, Málwá. That state, embracing the greater part of what we know as Central India, was thus independent at the accession of Akbar. So likewise was Khándesh: so also were the states of Rájpútána. These latter deserve a more detailed notice.

The exploits of the great Sanga Ráná have been incidentally referred to in the first chapter. The defeat of that prince by Bábar had greatly affected the power of Mewár, and when Sher Sháh drove Humáyún from India its chiefs had been compelled eventually to acknowledge the overlordship of the conqueror. But, during the disturbances which followed the death of Sher Sháh, they had recovered their independence, and at the accession of Akbar they still held their high place among the states of Rájpútána. Of the other states it may briefly be stated that the rulers of Jaipur had paid homage to the Mughal in the time of Bábar. The then Rájá, Bahármá, had assisted that prince with his forces, and had received from Humáyún, prior to his defeat by Sher Sháh, a high imperial title as ruler of Ámbar. The son of Bahármá, Bhagwán Dás, occupied the throne when Akbar won

Pánípat. Jodhpur, in those days, occupied a far higher position than did Jaipur. Its Rájá, Maldeo Singh, had given to the great Sher Sháh more trouble in the field than had any of his opponents. He had, however, refused an asylum to Humáyún when Humáyún was a fugitive. He was alive, independent, and the most powerful of all the princes of Rájpútána when Akbar ascended the throne of Delhi. Jaisalmer, Bíkáner, and the states on the borders of the desert were also independent. So likewise were the minor states of Rájpútána; so also was Sind; so also Múltán. Mewát and Baghelkhand owned no foreign master; but Gwalior, Orchha, Chanderí, Narwár, and Pannao suffered from their vicinity to Agra, and were more or less tributary, according to the leisure accruing to the conqueror to assert his authority.

But even in the provinces which owned the rule of the Muhammadan conqueror there was no cohesion. The king, sultan, or emperor, as he was variously called, was simply the lord of the nobles to whom the several provinces had been assigned. In his own court he ruled absolutely. He commanded the army in the field. But with the internal administration of the provinces he did not interfere. Each of these provinces was really, though not nominally, independent under its own viceroy.

According to all concurrent testimony the condition of the Hindu population, who constituted seven-eighths of the entire population of the provinces subject to Muhammadan rule, was one of contentment. They were allowed the free exercise of their religion, though they were liable to the *jizyia*, or capitation tax, imposed by Muhammadans on subject races of other faiths. But in all the departments of the Government the Hindu element was very strong. In most provinces the higher classes of this faith maintained a hereditary jurisdiction subordinate to the governor; and in time of war they supplied their quota of troops for service in the field.

Each province had thus a local army, ready to be placed at the disposal of the governor whenever he should deem it necessary. But, besides, and unconnected with this local army, he had almost always in the province a certain number of imperial troops, that is, of troops paid by the Sultán, and the command of which was vested in an officer nominated by the Sultán. This officer was, to a great extent, independent of the local governor, being directly responsible to the sovereign.

Theoretically, the administration of justice was perfect, for it was dispensed according to the Muhammadan principle that the state was dependent on the law. That law was administered by the Kázís or judges in conformity with a code which was the result of accumulated decisions based on the Kurán, but modified by the customs of the country. The Kází decided all matters of a civil character; all questions, in fact, which did not affect the safety of the state. But criminal cases were reserved to the jurisdiction of a body of men whose mode of procedure was practically undefined, and who, nominated and supported by the Crown, sometimes trenched on the authority of the Kází. The general contentment of the people would seem, however, to authorise the conclusion that, on the whole, the administration of justice was performed in a satisfactory manner. Time had welded together the interests of the families of the earlier Muhammadan immigrant and those of the Hindu inhabitant, and they both looked alike to the law to afford them such protection as was possible. In spite of the many wars, the general condition of the country was undoubtedly, if the native records may be trusted, very flourishing.

It is important to note, in considering the administration upon which we are now entering, that neither Bábar nor Humáyún had changed, to any material extent, the system of their Afghán predecessors in India. Bábar, indeed, had been accustomed to a system even more autocratic. Whether in Ferghaná, in Samarkand, or in Kábul, he had not only been the supreme lord in the capital, but also the feudal lord of the governors of provinces appointed by himself. Those governors, those chiefs of districts or of jaghírs, did indeed exercise an authority almost absolute within their respective domains. But they were always removable at the pleasure of the sovereign, and it became an object with them to administer on a plan which would secure substantial justice, or to maintain at the court agents who should watch over their interests with the ruling prince.

Similarly the army was composed of the personal retainers of the sovereign, swollen by the personal retainers of his chiefs and vassals and by the native tribes of the provinces occupied.

With Bábar, too, as with his son, the form of government had been a pure despotism. Free institutions were unknown. The laws passed by one sovereign might be annulled by his successor. The personal element, in fact, predominated everywhere. The only possible check on the will of the sovereign lay in successful rebellion. But if the sovereign were capable, successful rebellion was almost an impossibility. If he were just as well as capable, he discerned that the enforcement of justice constituted his surest safeguard against any rebellion.

Bábar, then, had found in the provinces of India which he had conquered a system prevailing not at all dissimilar in principle to that to which he had been accustomed in the more northern regions. Had he been disposed to change it, he had not the time. Nor had his successor either the time or the inclination. The system he had pondered over just prior to his death shows no radical advance in principle on that which had existed in Hindustán. He would have parcelled out the empire into six great divisions, of which Delhi, Agra, Kanauj, Jaunpur, Mándu, and Lahore should be the centres or capitals. Each of these would have been likewise great military commands, under a trusted general, whose army-corps should be so strong as to render him independent of outside aid : whilst the Emperor should give unity to the whole by visiting each division in turn with an army of twelve thousand horse, inspecting the local forces and examining the general condition of the province. The project was full of defects. It would have been a bad mode of administration even had the sovereign been always more capable than his generals. It could not have lasted a year had he been less so.

The sudden death of Humáyún came to interfere with, to prevent the execution of, this plan. Then followed the military events culminating in the triumph of Pánípat. That battle placed the young Akbar in a position his grandfather Bábar had occupied exactly thirty years before. Then, it had given Bábar the opportunity, of which he availed himself, to conquer North-western India, Behar, and part of Central India. A similar opportunity was given by the second battle of Pánípat to Akbar. On that field he had conquered the only enemy capable of coping with him seriously. As far as conquest then was concerned, his task was easy. But to make that conquest enduring, to consolidate the different provinces and the diverse nationalities, to devise and introduce a system so centralising as to make the influence of the Emperor permeate through every town and every province, and yet not sufficiently centralising to kill local traditions, local customs, local habits of thought,—that was a task his grandfather had never attempted; which, to his father, would have seemed an impossibility, even if it had occurred or had been presented to him. Yet, in their schemes, the absence of such a programme had left the empire conquered on the morrow of the Pánípat of 1526, an empire without root in the soil, dependent absolutely on continued military success; liable to be overthrown by the first strong gust; not one whit more stable than the empires of the Ghaznivides, the Ghors, the Khiljis, the Tughlaks, the Saiyids, the Lodís, which had preceded it. That it was not more stable was proved by the ease with which the empire founded by Bábar succumbed, in the succeeding reign, to the attacks of Sher Sháh. It may be admitted that if Bábar had been immortal he might possibly have beaten back Sher Sháh. But that admission serves to prove my argument. Bábar was a very able general. So likewise was Sher Khán. Humáyún was flighty, versatile, and unpractical; as a general of but small account. It is possible that the Sher Khán who triumphed over Humáyún might have been beaten by Bábar. But that only proves that the system introduced by Bábar was the system to which he had been accustomed all his life—the system which had alternately lost and won for him Ferghána and Samarkand; which had given him Kábul, and, a few years later, India; the system of the rule of the strongest. Nowhere, neither in Ferghána, nor in Samarkand, nor in Kábul, nor in the Punjab, nor in India, had it shot down any roots. It was in fact impossible it could do so, for it possessed no germinating power.

And now, at the close of 1556, the empire won and lost and won again was in the hands of a boy, reared in the school of adversity and trial, one month over fourteen years [1]. Pánípat had given him India. Young as he was, he had seen much of affairs. He had been constantly consulted by his father: he had undergone a practical military education under Bairám, the first commander of the day: he had governed the Punjab for over six months. But it was as an administrator as well as a conqueror that he was now about to be tried. In that respect neither the example of his father, nor the precepts of Bairám, could influence him for good. So far as can be known, he had already displayed the germs of a judgment prompt to meet difficulties, a disposition inclined to mercy. He had refused to slay Hemu. But other qualities were required for the task now opening before him. Let us examine by the light of subsequent transactions what were his qualifications for the task.

[1] Akbar was born the 15th October, 1542. The second battle of Pánípat was fought the 5th November, 1556.

CHAPTER X.

THE TUTELAGE UNDER BAIRÁM KHÁN

FIRST, as to his outward appearance. 'Akbar,' wrote his son, the Emperor Jahángír[1], 'was of middling stature, but with a tendency to be tall; he had a wheat-colour complexion, rather inclining to be dark than fair, black eyes and eyebrows, stout body, open forehead and chest, long arms and hands. There was a fleshy wart, about the size of a small pea, on the left side of his nose, which appeared exceedingly beautiful, and which was considered very auspicious by physiognomists, who said that it was a sign of immense riches and increasing prosperity. He had a very loud voice, and a very elegant and pleasant way of speech. His manners and habits were quite different from those of other persons, and his visage was full of godly dignity.' Other accounts confirm, in its essentials, this description. Elphinstone writes of him as 'a strongly built and handsome man, with an agreeable expression of countenance, and very captivating manners,' and as having been endowed with great personal strength. He was capable of enduring great fatigue; was fond of riding, of walking, of shooting, of

---

[1] Sir Henry Elliot's *History of India, as told by its own Historians*, vol. vi. p. 290.

hunting, and of all exercises requiring strength and skill. His courage was that calm, cool courage which is never thrown off its balance, but rather shines with its greatest lustre under difficulty and danger. Though ready to carry on war, especially for objects which he deemed essential to the welfare of the empire or for the common weal, he did not rejoice in it. Indeed, he infinitely preferred applying himself to the development of those administrative measures which he regarded as the true foundation of his authority. War, then, to him was nothing more than a necessary evil. We shall find throughout his career that he did not wage a single war which he did not consider to be necessary to the completion and safety of his civil system. He had an affectionate disposition, was true to his friends, very capable of inspiring affection in others, disliked bloodshed, was always anxious to temper justice with mercy, preferred forgiveness to revenge, though, if the necessities of the case required it, he could be stern and could steel his heart against its generous promptings. Like all large-hearted men he was fond of contributing to the pleasures of others. Generosity was thus a part of his nature, and, even when the recipient of his bounties proved unworthy, he was more anxious to reform him than regretful of his liberality. For civil administration he had a natural inclination, much preferring the planning of a system which might render the edifice his arms were erecting suitable to the yearnings of the people to the planning of a

TUTELAGE UNDER BAIRÁM KHÁN

campaign. On all the questions which have affected mankind in all ages, and which affect them still, the questions of religion, of civil polity, of the administration of justice, he had an open mind, absolutely free from prejudice, eager to receive impressions. Born and bred a Muhammadan, he nevertheless consorted freely and on equal terms with the followers of Buddha, of Bráhma, of Zoroaster, and of Jesus. It has been charged against him that in his later years he disliked learned men, and even drove them from his court. It would be more correct to say that he disliked the prejudice, the superstition, and the obstinate adherence to the beliefs in which they had been educated, of the professors who frequented his court. He disliked, that is, the weaknesses and the foibles of the learned, and when these were carried to excess, he dispensed with their attendance at his court. What he was in other respects will be discovered by the reader for himself in the last chapter of this book. Sufficient, I hope, has been stated to give him some idea of the characteristics of the latent capacity of the young prince, who, fourteen years old, had under the tutelage of Bairám Khán won the battle of Pánípat, and had marched from the field directly, without a halt, upon Delhi. Few, if any, of those about him knew then the strength of his character or the resources of his intellect. Certainly, his Atálik, Bairám, did not understand him, or he would neither have assassinated Tardí Beg in his tent at Sirhind, nor have suggested to the young prince to plunge his sword into the body of the captured Hemu. But both Bairám and the other nobles of the court and army were not long kept in ignorance of the fact that in the son of Humáyún they had, not a boy who might be managed, but a master who would be obeyed.

Akbar remained one month at Delhi. He sent thence a force into Mewát to pursue the broken army of Hemu and to gain the large amount of treasure it was conveying. In this short campaign his general, Pir Muhammad Khán of Sherwán, at the time a follower of Bairám but afterwards persecuted by him[1], was eminently successful. Akbar then marched upon and recovered Agra.

But his conquests south of the Sutlej were not safe so long as the Punjab was not secure. And, as we have seen, he had been forced to leave at Mánkót, driven back but not overcome, a determined enemy of his House in the person of Sikandar Sur. In March of the following year (1557) he received information that the advanced guard of the troops he had left in the Punjab had been defeated by that prince some forty miles from Lahore. Noblemen who came from the Punjab told him that the business was very serious, as Sikandar had made sure of a very strong base at Mánkót, whence he might emerge to annoy even though he were defeated in the field, and that his victory had encouraged his partisans. Akbar recognised all the force of the argument, and resolved to put in force a maxim which constituted the great

[1] *Ain-i-Akbari* (Blochmann's Edition), pp. 324-5.

strength of his reign, that if a thing were to be done at all, it should be done thoroughly. He accordingly marched straight on Lahore, and, finding Lahore safe, from that capital into Jálandhar, where his enemy was maintaining his ground. On the approach of Akbar, Sikandar retreated towards the Siwáliks, and threw himself into Mánkót. There Akbar besieged him.

The siege lasted six months. Then, pressed by famine and weakened by desertions, Sikandar sent some of his nobles to ask for terms. Akbar acceded to his request that his enemy might be allowed to retire to Bengal, leaving his son as a hostage that he would not again war against the Emperor. The fort then surrendered, and Akbar returned to Lahore; spent four months and fourteen days there to arrange the province, and then marched on Delhi. As he halted at Jálandhar, there took place the marriage of Bairám Khán with a cousin of the late emperor, Humáyún. This marriage had been arranged by Humáyún, and to the young prince his father's wishes on such subjects were a law. Akbar re-entered Delhi on the 15th of March, 1558. Bairám Khán was still, in actual management of affairs, the Atálik, the tutor, of the sovereign, and he continued to be so during the two years that followed, 1558 and 1559. It was not easy for a young boy to shake off all at once the influence of a great general under whom he had been placed to learn his trade, and possibly Akbar, though he did not approve many of the acts authorised in his name by his Atálik, did not feel himself strong enough to throw off the yoke. But the removal by the strong hand of men whom Akbar liked, but who had incurred without reason the enmity of Bairám, gradually estranged the heart of the sovereign from his too autocratic minister. The estrangement, once begun, rapidly increased. Bairám did not recognise the fact that every year was developing the strong points in the character of his master; that he was adding experience and knowledge of affairs to the great natural gifts with which he had been endowed. He still continued to see in him the boy of whom he had been the tutor, whose armies he had led to victory, and whose dominions he was administering. The exercise of power without a check had made the exercise of such power necessary to him, and he continued to wield it with all the self-sufficiency of a singularly determined nature.

Round every young ruler there will be men who will never fail to regard the exercise by another of authority rightly pertaining to him as a grievous wrong to the ruler and to themselves. It is not necessary to inquire into the motives of such men. For one reason or another, often doubtless of a selfish, rarely of a pure and disinterested nature, they desire the young and rightful master of the State to be the dispenser of power and patronage. That there was a cluster of such men about Akbar, of men who disliked Bairám, who had been injured by him, who expected from the prince favours which they could not hope to obtain from the minister, is certain. Female influence was also brought to bear on the mind of the sovereign. His nurse, who had attended on him from his cradle until after his accession, and who subsequently became the chief of his harem, urged upon him that the time had arrived when he should take the administration into his own hands. Akbar was not unwilling. He was in his eighteenth year. The four years he had lived since Pánípat had restored to him part of the inheritance of his father, had been utilised by him in a manner calculated to develop and strengthen his natural qualities. But, though he saw and disliked the tendency to cruelty and arbitrary conduct often displayed by his chief minister, he had that regard for Bairám which a generous heart instinctively feels for the man who has been his tutor from his childhood. Experience, too, had given him so thorough an insight into the character of Bairám that he could not but be sensible that any breach with him must be a complete breach; that he must rid himself of him in a manner which would render it impossible for him to aspire to the exercise of any power whatever. Bairám, he knew, would have the whole authority, or it would be unsafe to entrust him with any.

Various circumstances occurred in the beginning of 1560 which determined Akbar to take into his own hands the reins of government. He went therefore from Agra to Delhi resolved to announce this determination to his minister. Bairám himself had more than once given an example of the mode in which he rid himself of a rival or a noble whom he hated. His methods were the dagger or the sword. But such a remedy was abhorrent to the pure mind of the young Emperor. Nor—so far as can be gathered from the records of the period—had anyone dared to whisper to him a proposal of that character. The course which his mother and his nurse had alike suggested was to propose to the minister in a manner which would make the proposition have all the effect of a command, an honourable exile to Mekka. Bairám had often publicly declared that he was longing for the opportunity when he could safely resign his political burden into the hands of others and make the pilgrimage which would ensure salvation. Akbar then, anxious to prevent any armed resistance, on arriving at Delhi, issued a proclamation in which he declared that he had assumed the administration of affairs, and forbade obedience to any orders but to those issued by himself. He sent a message to this effect to his minister, and suggested in it the desirability of his making a pilgrimage to Mekka[1]. Bairám had heard of Akbar's determination before the message reached him, and had quitted Agra on his way

---

[1] The message ran: 'As I was fully assured of your honesty and fidelity I left all important affairs of State to your charge, and thought only of my own pleasures. I have now determined to take the reins of government into my own hands, and it is desirable that you should now make the pilgrimage to Mekka, upon which you have been so long intent. A suitable jagír out of the parganás of Hindustán shall be assigned to your maintenance, the revenues of which shall be transmitted to you by your agents.' Elliot, vol. v. p. 264.

to the western coast. He was evidently very angry, and bent on mischief, for, on reaching Biána, he set free some turbulent nobles who had been there confined. He received there Akbar's message, and continued thence his journey to Nagaur in Rájpútána, accompanied only by nobles who were related to him, and by their respective escorts. From Nagaur, by the hand of one of these, he despatched to the Emperor, as a token of submission to his will, his banner, his kettle-drums, and all other marks of nobility. Akbar, who had been assured that Bairám would most certainly attempt to rouse the Punjab against him, had marched with an army towards that province, and was at Jhajhar, in the Rohtak district, when the insignia reached him. He conferred them upon a former adherent of Bairám's, but who in more recent times had lived under the displeasure of that nobleman, and commissioned him to follow his late master and see that he embarked for Mekka. Bairám was greatly irritated at this proceeding, and turning short to Bíkáner, placed his family under the care of his adopted son and broke out into rebellion. But he had to learn the wide difference of the situation of a rebel against the Mughal, and the trusted chief officer of the Mughal. On reaching Dipálpur, the news overtook him that his adopted son had proved false to his trust and had turned against him. Resolved, however, to rouse the Jálandhar Duáb, he pushed on for that well-known locality, only to encounter on its borders the army of the Governor of the Punjab, Atjah Khán. In the battle that followed Bairám was defeated, and fled to Tilwára on the Sutlej, thirty miles to the west of Ludhiána. Akbar, who had been on his track when his lieutenant encountered and defeated him, followed his late Atálik, and reduced him to such straits that Bairám threw himself on his mercy. Then Akbar, remembering the great services he had rendered, pardoned him, and, furnishing him with a large sum of money, despatched him on the road to Mekka. Bairám reached Gujarát in safety, was well received there by the Governor, and was engaged in making his preparations to quit India, when he was assassinated [1] by a Loháni Afghán whose father had been killed at the battle of Machcíwára. Akbar, meanwhile, had returned to Delhi (November 9, 1560). He rested there a few days and then pushed on to Agra, there to execute the projects he had formed for the conquest, the union, the consolidation of the provinces he was resolved to weld into an empire. His reign, indeed, in the sense of ruling alone without a minister who assumed the airs of a master, commenced really from this date. The Atálik, who had monopolised the power of the State, was gone, and the future of the country depended now entirely upon the genius of the sovereign.

[1] The motive attributed to the assassin was simply revenge. Bairám was stabbed in the back so that the point of the long dagger came out at his breast. 'With an Allahu Akbar' (God is great) 'on his lips he died,' writes Blochmann in his *Ain-i-Akbari*. His son was provided for by Akbar.

CHAPTER XI

Chronicle of the Reign

THE position in India, in the sixth year of Akbar's reign, dating from the battle of Pánípat, but the first of his personal rule, may thus be summarised. He held the Punjab and the North-western Provinces, as we know those provinces, including Gwalior and Ajmere to the west, Lucknow, and the remainder of Oudh, including Allahábád, as far as Jaunpur, to the east. Benares, Chanar, and the provinces of Bengal and Behar, were still held by princes of the house of Sur, or by the representatives of other Afghán families. The whole of Southern India, the greater part of Western India, were outside the territories which acknowledged his sway.

There can be little doubt that, during the five years of his tutelage under Bairám, Akbar had deeply considered the question of how to govern India so as to unite the hearts of the princes and people under the protecting arm of a sovereign whom they should regard as national. The question was encumbered with difficulties. Four centuries of the rule of Muhammadan sovereigns who had made no attempt to cement into one bond of mutual interests the various races who inhabited the peninsula, each ruling on the principle of temporary superiority, each falling as soon as a greater power presented itself, had not only introduced a conviction of the ephemeral character of the successive dynasties, and of the actual dynasty for the time being. It had also left scattered all over the country, from Bengal to Gujarát, a number of pretenders, offshoots of families which had reigned, every one of whom regarded the Mughal as being only a temporary occupant of the supreme seat of power, to be replaced; as fortune might direct, possibly by one of themselves, possibly by a new invader. This conviction of the ephemeral character of the actual rule was increased by the recollection of the ease with which Humáyún had been overthrown. Defeated at Kanauj, he had quitted India leaving not a trace of the thirteen years of Mughal sway, not a single root in the soil.

These were facts which Akbar had recognised. The problem, to his mind, was how to act so as to efface from the minds of princes and people these recollections; to conquer that he might unite; to introduce, as he conquered, principles so acceptable to all classes, to the prince as well as to the peasant, that they should combine to regard him as the protecting father, the unit necessary to ward off from them evil, the assurer to them of the exercise of their immemorial rights and privileges, the assertor of the right of the ablest, independently of his religion, or his caste, or his nationality, to exercise command under himself, the maintainer of equal laws, equal justice, for all classes. Such became, as his mind developed, the principles of Akbar. He has been accused, he was accused in his life-time, by bigoted Muhammadan writers, of arrogating to himself the attributes of the Almighty. This charge is only true in the sense that, in an age and in a country in which might had been synonymous with right, he did pose as the messenger from Heaven, the representative on earth of the power of God, to introduce union, toleration, justice, mercy, equal rights, amongst the peoples of Hindustán.

His first aim was to bring all India under one sceptre, and to accomplish this task in a great measure by enlisting in its favour the several races which he desired to bring within the fold. I have thought it advisable for the fuller comprehension of his system to treat the subject in its two aspects, the physical and the moral. This chapter, then, will chronicle the successive attempts to bring under one government and one form of law the several states into which India was then divided. The chapter that follows will deal more particularly with the moral aspect of the question.

It would be tedious, in a work like this, to follow Akbar in all the details of his conquests in India. It will suffice to record that, during the first year of his own personal administration and the sixth of his actual reign, he re-attached Málwá to his dominions. Later in the season his generals repelled an attempt made by the Afghán ruler of Chanar and the country east of the Karamnásá to attack Jaunpur, whilst Akbar himself, marching by way of Kálpi, crossed there the Jumna, and proceeded as far as Karrah, not far from Allahábád, on the right bank of the Ganges. There he was joined by his generals who held Jaunpur, and thence he returned to Agra. The year, at its close, witnessed the siege of Merta, a town in the Jodhpur state, then of considerable importance, beyond Ajmere, and seventy-six miles to the north-east of the city of Jodhpur. This expedition was directed by Akbar from Ajmere where he was then residing, though he confided the execution of it to his generals. The place was defended with great energy by the Rájpút garrison, but, in the spring of the following year it was surrendered on condition that the garrison should march out with their horses and arms, but should leave behind all their property and effects.

In the same year in which Merta fell (1562), the generals of Akbar in Málwá, pushing westward, added the cities of Bijágarh and Burhánpur on the Tápti to his dominions. The advantage proved, however, to be the forerunner of a calamity, for the dispossessed governors of those towns, combining with the expelled Afghán ruler of Málwá, and aided by the zamíndárs of the country, long accustomed to their rule, made a desperate attack upon the imperial forces. These, laden with the spoils of Burhánpur, were completely defeated. For the moment Málwá was lost, but the year did not expire before the

Mughal generals, largely reinforced, had recovered it. The Afghán noble, whilom Governor of Málwá, after some wanderings, threw himself on the mercy of Akbar, and, to use the phrase of the chronicler, 'sought a refuge from the frowns of fortune.' Akbar made him a commander of one thousand, and a little later promoted him to the mansab (dignity) of a commander of two thousand. He died in the service of his new sovereign. The reader will not fail to notice how the principle of winning over his enemies by assuring to them rank, position, and consideration, instead of driving them to despair, was constantly acted upon by Akbar. His design was to unite, to weld together. Hence he was always generous to the vanquished. He would bring their strength into his strength, instead of allowing it to become a strength outside his own. He would make those who would in the first instance be inclined to resist him feel that conquest by him, or submission to him, would in no way impair their dignity, but, ultimately, would increase it. We shall note the working of this principle more clearly when we come to describe his dealings with the several chiefs of Rájpútána.

A tragic event came to cloud the spring of the eighth year of the reign of Akbar. I have referred already to the regard and affection he entertained for the lady who had been his nurse in his infancy, and who had watched his tender years. It was to a great extent upon her advice that he had acted in dealing with Bairám. She had a splendid provision in the palace, and Akbar had provided handsomely for her sons. The eldest of these, however, fired with jealousy at the elevation of men whose equal or superior he considered himself to be, and goaded probably by men of a like nature to his own, assassinated the Prime Minister as he was sitting in his public office; then, trusting to the favour which Akbar had always displayed towards his family and himself, went and stood at the door of the harem. But for such a man, and for such an act, Akbar had no mercy. The assassin was cut to pieces, and his dead body was hurled over the parapet into the moat below. Those who had incited him, dreading lest their complicity should be discovered, fled across the Jumna, but they were caught, sent back to Agra, and were ultimately pardoned. The mother of the chief culprit died forty days later from grief at her son's conduct.

For some time previously the condition of a portion of the Punjab had been the cause of some anxiety to Akbar. The Gakkhars, a tribe always turbulent, and the chiefs of which had never heartily accepted the Mughal sovereigns, had set at defiance the orders issued for the disposal of their country by Akbar. They had refused, that is, to acknowledge the governor he had nominated. The Gakkhars inhabited, as their descendants inhabit now, that part of the Punjab which may be described as forming the north-eastern part of the existing district of Ráwal Pindí. To enforce his orders Akbar sent thither an army, and this army, after some sharp fighting, succeeded in restoring order.

The chief of the Gakkhars was taken prisoner, and died whilst still under surveillance. Akbar caused to be repressed likewise disturbances which had arisen in Kábul, and met with promptitude a conspiracy formed by the favourite of Humáyún, Abul Má'alí, whose pretensions he had more than once put down, but who was now returning, puffed up with pride, from a pilgrimage to Mekka. Concerting a plan with another discontented noble, Abul Má'alí fell upon a detachment of the royal army near Nárnul, and destroyed it. Akbar sent troops in pursuit of him, and Abul Má'alí, terrified, fled to Kábul, and wrote thence letters full of penitence to Akbar. Ultimately, that is, early the following year, Abul Má'alí was taken prisoner in Badakshán, and strangled.

Up to the spring of 1564 Akbar had not put into execution the designs which he cherished for establishing the Mughal power in the provinces to the east of Allahábád. Chanar, then considered the key of those eastern territories, was held by a slave of the Adel dynasty. This slave, threatened by one of Akbar's generals, wrote a letter to the Emperor offering to surrender it. Akbar sent two of his nobles to take over the fortress, and to them it was surrendered. The possession of Chanar offered likewise an opening into the district of Narsinghpur, governed by a Rání, who held her court in the fortress of Chaurágarh. Against her marched the Mughal general, defeated her in a pitched battle, and added Narsinghpur and portions of what is now styled the district of

Hoshangábád to the imperial dominions. In the hot weather of the same year, Akbar, under the pretext of hunting, started for the central districts, when he was surprised by the advent of the rainy season, and with some difficulty made his way across the swollen streams to Narwár, then a flourishing city boasting a circumference of twenty miles. After hunting for some days in the vicinity of that city he pushed on towards Málwá, and passing through Ráwa and Sarangpur, proceeded towards the famous Mándu, twenty-six miles south-west of Mhow. The Governor of Mándu, an Uzbek noble placed there by Akbar, conscious that the Emperor had grounds for dissatisfaction with him, and placing no trust in a reassuring message sent him by his sovereign, abandoned the city as Akbar approached, and took the field with his followers. Akbar sent a force after him which pursued him to the confines of Gujarát, and took from him his horses, his elephants, and his wives.

The reception accorded to Akbar in Mándu was of the most gratifying character. The zamíndárs of the neighbouring districts crowded in to pay homage, and the King of distant Khándesh sent an embassy to greet him. Akbar received the ambassador with distinction. It deserves to be mentioned, as a characteristic feature of the customs of those times, that when Akbar honoured the ambassador with a farewell audience, he placed in his hand a firmán addressed to his master, directing him to send to Mándu any one of his daughters whom he might consider worthy to attend upon the Emperor. The native historian adds: 'when Mubárak Sháh,' the ruler of Khándesh, 'received this gracious communication, he was greatly delighted, and he sent his daughter with a suitable retinue and paraphernalia to his Majesty, esteeming it a great favour to be allowed to do so.' After a short stay at Mándu, Akbar returned to Agra, by way of Ujjain, Sarangpur, Siprí, Narwár, and Gwalior. During the ensuing cold weather he spent a great part of his time hunting in the Gwalior districts.

There can be but few travellers from the West to India who have not admired the fortress, built of red sandstone, which is one of the sights of Agra. At the time of the accession of Akbar there was at Agra simply a citadel built of brick, ugly in form and ruinous from decay. Akbar had for some time past resolved to build on its ruins a fortress which should be worthy of the ruler of an empire, and in the late spring of 1565 he determined on the plans, and gave the necessary orders. The work was carried on under the direction of Kásím Khán, a distinguished officer whom Akbar had made a commander of three thousand. The building of the fortress took eight years of continuous labour, and the cost was thirty-five lakhs of rupees. It is built, as I have said, of red sandstone, the stones being well joined together and fastened to each other by iron rings which pass through them. The foundation everywhere reaches water.

The year did not close without an event which afforded Akbar the opportunity of displaying his decision and prompt action in sudden emergencies. I have shown how, on his visit to Mándu, the Uzbek governor of that city had taken fright and rushed into rebellion; how Akbar had caused him to be pursued and punished. The treatment of the rebel, though not unduly severe, had spread in the minds of the Uzbek nobles at the court and in the army the impression that the Emperor disliked men of that race, and three or four of them combined to give him a lesson. The rebellion broke out in the autumn of the year at Jaunpur, the governor of which the Uzbeks had secured to their interests. Akbar was engaged in elephant-hunting at Narwár when the news reached him.

He immediately despatched his ablest general with the troops that were available to aid his loyal officers, whilst he should collect further troops to follow. He marched about ten days later, reached Kanauj, received there the submission of one of the rebel leaders, remained there ten days, waiting till the river, swollen by the rainfall, should subside. Learning then that the chief who was the head of the rebellion had proceeded to Lucknow, he promptly followed him thither with a small but chosen body of troops, and marching incessantly for four-and-twenty hours, came in sight of that city on the morning of the second day. As he approached, the rebels fled with such speed that the horses of the Emperor and his retinue, completely knocked up with their long march, could not follow them. The rebel chief then fell back rapidly on Jaunpur, and joining there his colleagues, quitted that place with them, and crossing the Gogra at the ford of Narhan, forty miles west-north-west of Chaprá, remained encamped there. Thence they despatched agents into Bengal to implore the aid of the king of that country.

Meanwhile, one imperial army, led by a general anxious for a bloodless termination to the dispute, had arrived in front of them, whilst another, commanded by a fiery and resólute leader, was marching up from Rájpútána. The negotiations which the peaceful general had commenced had almost concluded, when the fiery leader arrived, and, declaring the negotiations to be a fraud, insisted upon fighting. In the battle which followed the imperial forces were defeated, and fled to re-assemble the day following at Shergarh.

Before this battle had been fought Akbar had confirmed the peace negotiations with the rebels, and he was not moved from his resolution when he heard of their victory over his army. He said: 'their faults have been forgiven,' and he sent instructions to his Amírs to return to court. He then marched himself to Chanar, alike to plan works for the strengthening of the fortress; to hunt elephants in the Mírzápur jungles; and to await the further action of the rebels he had pardoned with arms in their hands. The experiment was not one to be repeated, for, flushed with their success, the rebel chiefs broke out anew. Akbar, however, by a skilful disposition of his forces, compelled their submission, and received them back to favour. In the course of this year the imperial generals had taken the fortress of Rotás, in Behar, and ambassadors, sent on a mission to the king of Orissa, had returned laden with splendid presents.

The spring of the year 1566 found the Emperor back at Agra. The native historians record that in these times of peace his great delight was to spend the evening in the game of cháugan. Cháugan is the modern polo, which was carried to Europe from India. But Akbar, whilst playing it in the daytime in the manner in which it is now played all over the world, devised a method of playing it on the dark nights which supervene so quickly on the daylight in India. For this purpose he had balls made of palás wood—a wood which is very light and which burns for a long time, and set them on fire. He had the credit of being the keenest cháugan-player of his time.

From this pleasure Akbar was roused by the news of successful rebellions at Kábul and at Lahore. He marched with all haste towards the close of the year in the direction of the Sutlej, reached Delhi in ten days; thence marched to Sirhind; and thence joyfully to Lahore. Thence he despatched his generals to drive the rebels across the Indus. This they accomplished, and returned. The troubles at Kábul were at the same time appeased: but, as a counter-irritant, the absence of the Emperor so far in the north-west brought about rebellion at Jaunpur. It was clear that up to this time—the end of 1566—Akbar had been unable successfully to grapple with the important question how to establish a permanent government in Hindustán. The eleventh year of his reign, counting from the battle of Pánípat, was now closing, and he had fixed so few roots in the soil that it was certain that, should a fatal accident befall him, the succession would again be decided by the sword. The beginning of the year 1567 found him still at Lahore, engaged in hunting and similar pleasures. He was roused from these diversions by the intelligence that the Uzbek nobles whom he had pardoned, had taken advantage of his absence to break out again. Accordingly he quitted Lahore on the 22nd of March, and began his return-march to Ágra. On reaching Thuneswar, in Sirhind, he was greatly entertained by a fight between two sects of Hindu devotees, the Jogís and the Suniásís, for the possession of the rich harvest of gold, jewels, and stuffs, brought to the shrine of the saint by pious pilgrims. Another sign of the instability of his rule awaited him at Delhi, for he found that a state prisoner had eluded the vigilance of the governor, and that the governor, apprehensive of the imperial displeasure, had quitted the city, and broken into rebellion.

Nor, even when he reached Agra, did more reassuring tidings await him. The country about Kanauj was in a state of rebellion, and it was clear to him that many of his nobles could not be trusted. In this emergency he marched to Bhojpur, in the Rái Bareli district, thence to Rái Bareli. There he learned that the rebels had crossed the Ganges with the object of proceeding towards Kálpi. There had been heavy rains and the country was flooded, but Akbar, eager for action, despatched his main forces to Karrah whilst he hastened with a body of chosen troops to Mánikpur, midway between Partábgarh and Allahábád. There he crossed the river on an elephant, pushed on with great celerity, caught the rebels at the village of Mánikpur, and completely defeated them. The principal leaders of the revolt were killed during or after the battle. From the battle-field, Akbar marched to Allahábád, then called by its ancient name of Pryága. After a visit to Benares and to Jaunpur, in the course of which he settled the country, he returned to Agra.

Deeming his eastern territories now secure, Akbar turned his attention to Rájpútána. The most ancient of all the rulers of the kingdoms in that large division of Western India was Udai Singh, Ráná of Mewár, a man possessing a character in which weakness was combined with great obstinacy. His principal stronghold was the famous fortress of Chitor, a fortress which had indeed succumbed to Allah-ud-dín Khilji in 1303, but which had regained the reputation of being impregnable. It stands on a high oblong hill above the river Banás, the outer wall of the fortifications adapting itself to the shape of the hill. It was defended by an army of about seven thousand Rájpúts, good soldiers, and commanded by a true and loyal captain. It was supplied with provisions and abundance of water, and was in all respects able to stand a long siege.

Akbar himself sat down before the fortress, whilst he sent another body of troops to make conquests in the vicinity, for the Ráná, despairing of success, had fled to the jungles. But if he pressed the siege vigorously, the Rájpúts defended themselves with equal courage and obstinacy. Never had Akbar met such sturdy warriors. As their pertinacity increased, so likewise did his pride and resolution. At length the breach was reported practicable, and on a night in the month of March, Akbar ordered the assault. He had a stand erected for himself, whence he could watch and direct the operations. As he sat there, his gun in his hand, he observed the gallant Rájpúts assembling in the breach, led by their capable commander, prepared to give his troops a warm reception. The distance between his stand and the breach was, as the crow flies, but short, for the river alone ran between the two.

By the light of the torches, Akbar easily recognised the Rájpút general, and believing him to be within distance, he fired and killed him on the spot. This fortunate shot, despatched whilst the hostile parties were approaching one another, so discouraged the Rájpúts, that at the critical moment they made but a poor defence. They rallied indeed subsequently, but it was too late, and though they then exerted themselves to the utmost, they could not regain the lost advantage. When the day dawned, Chitor was in the possession of Akbar. In gratitude for its victory Akbar, in pursuance of a vow he had made before he began the siege, made a pilgrimage on foot to the mausoleum of the first Muhammadan saint of India, Ma'inu-i-din Chisti of Sijistan, on the summit of the hill of Ajmere. He had not then emancipated himself from his early training. He remained ten days at Ajmere, and returned thence to Agra by way of Mewát.

Akbar spent the spring and rainy season at Agra. He then designed the conquest of the strong fortress of Rantambhor in Jaipur, but whilst the army he had raised for this purpose was on its march, disturbances in Gujarát, followed by an invasion of Central India from that side, compelled Akbar to divert his troops to meet that danger. He then decided to march in person with another army against Rantambhor. This he did early in the following year (1569). As soon as he had compelled the surrender of the fortress, he returned to Agra, stopping on the way a week at Ajmere, to visit once again the mausoleum of the saint.

This year he founded Fatehpur-Síkrí, the magnificent ruins of which compel, in the present day, the admiration of the traveller. The story is thus told by the author of the Tabakat. After stating that Akbar had had two sons, twins, neither of whom had lived, he goes on to say that Shaikh Salím Chisti, who resided at Síkrí, twenty-two miles to the south-west of Agra, had promised him a son who should survive. Full of the hope of the fulfilment of this promise, Akbar, after his return from Rantambhor, had paid the saint several visits, remaining there ten to twenty days on each occasion; eventually he built a palace there on the summit of a rising ground; whilst the saint commenced a new monastery and a fine mosque, near the royal mansion. The nobles of the court, fired by these examples, began then to build houses for themselves.

Whilst his own palace was building one of his wives became pregnant, and Akbar conveyed her to the dwelling of the holy man. When, somewhat later, he had conquered Gujarát he gave to the favoured town the prefix 'Fatehpur' (City of victory). The place has since been known in history by the joint names of Fatehpur-Síkrí. Towards the end of the year his wife, whom he had sent to reside at Síkrí, gave birth to a son at the house of the saint, who is known in history as the Emperor Jahángír, though called after the saint by the name of Salím. His mother was a Rájpút princess of Jodhpur. To commemorate this event Akbar made of Fatehpur-Síkrí a permanent royal abode; built a stone fortification round it, and erected some splendid edifices. He then made another pilgrimage on foot to the mausoleum of the saint on the Ajmere hill. Having paid his devotions he proceeded to Delhi.

Early the following year Akbar marched into Rájpútána and halted at Nagaur, in Jodhpur. There he received the homage of the son of the Rájá of that principality, then the most powerful in Rájpútána, and that of the Rájá of Bíkáner and his son. As a tribute of his appreciation of the loyalty of the latter, Akbar took the Rájá's daughter in marriage. He amused himself for some time at Nagaur in hunting the wild asses which at that time there abounded, and then proceeded to Dipálpur in the Punjab. There he held a magnificent durbar, and then, with the dawn of the new year, proceeded to Lahore. After settling the affairs of the Punjab, he returned to Fatehpur-Síkrí with the intention of devoting the coming year to the conquest of Gujarát.

The province of Gujarát in Western India included, in the time of Akbar, the territories and districts of Surat, Broach, Kaira, Ahmadábád, a great part of what is now Baroda, the territories now represented by the Mahi Kántha and Rewá Kántha agencies, the Panch Mahas, Pálanpur, Rádhanpur, Balisna, Cambay, Khandeah, and the great peninsula of Káthiáwár. This agglomeration of territories had for a long time had no legitimate master. Parcelled out into districts, each of which was ruled by a Muhammadan noble alien to the great bulk of the population, it had been for years the scene of constant civil war, the chiefs grinding the peasantry to obtain the means wherewith to obtain the supreme mastery. Sometimes, fired by information of the weakness of an adjoining province, the chiefs would combine to make temporary raids. The result was that Gujarát had become the focus of disorder. The people were oppressed, and the petty tyrants who ruled over them were bent only on seeking advantages at the expense of others. Akbar had long felt the results of this anarchy, and he resolved now to put an end to it for ever.

The expedition of Akbar to Gujarát is the most famous military exploit of his reign. He was resolved that there should be no mistake either in its plan or in its execution. For the first time since he had become ruler of the greater part of India he felt reasonably secure, during the probable duration of the expedition, of the conduct of his nobles and his vassals. He set out from Fatehpur-Síkrí at the head of his army in September, 1572, and marching by Sanganer, eighteen miles south of Jaipur, reached Ajmere the middle of October. There he stayed two days to visit the mausoleum of the saint, then, having sent an advanced guard of ten thousand horse to feel the way, followed with the bulk of the army, and marched on Nagaur, seventy-five miles to the north-east of Jodhpur. On reaching Nagaur a courier arrived with the information that a son, later known as Prince Dányál, had been born to him. He spent there fourteen days in arranging for the supplies of his army, then pushing on, reached Patan, on the Saraswatí, in November, and Ahmadábád early in the following month. In the march between the two places he had received the submission of the chief who claimed to be supreme lord of Gujarát, but whose authority was barely nominal. At Ahmadábád, then the first city in Gujarát, Akbar was proclaimed Emperor of Western India.

There remained, however, to be dealt with many of the chieftains, all unwilling to renounce the authority they possessed. Amongst these were the rulers of Broach, of Baroda, and of Surat. No sooner, then, had the Emperor arranged matters at Ahmadábád for the good order of the country, than he set out for Cambay, and reached it in five days. There, we are told by the historians, he gazed for the first time on the sea. After a stay there of nearly a week, he marched, in two days, to Baroda. There he completed his arrangements for the administration of the country, appointing Ahmadábád to be the capital, and nominating a governor from amongst the nobles who had accompanied him from Agra. Thence, too, he despatched a force to secure Broach and Surat. Information having reached him that the chief of Broach had murdered the principal adherent of the Mughal cause in that city, and had then made for the interior, passing within fifteen miles of Baroda, Akbar dashed after him with what troops he had in hand, and on the second night came in sight of his camp at Sársa, on the further side of a little river.

Akbar had then with him but forty horsemen, and, the river being fordable, he endeavoured to conceal his men until reinforcements should arrive. These came up in the night to the number of sixty, and with his force, now increased to a total number of a hundred, Akbar forded the river to attack ten times their number. The rebel leader, instead of awaiting the attack in the town, made for the open, to give a better chance to his preponderating numbers. Akbar carried the town with a rush, and then dashed in pursuit. But the country was intersected by lanes, bordered on both sides by cactus hedges, and the horsemen of Akbar were driven back into a position in which but three of them could fight abreast, the enemy being on either side of the cactus hedges. The Emperor was in front of his men, having by his side the gallant Rájpút prince, Rájá Bhagwán Dás of Jaipur, whose sister he had married, and the Rájá's nephew and destined successor, Mán Singh, one of the most brilliant warriors of the day. The three were in the greatest danger, for the enemy made tremendous efforts to break in upon them. But the cactus hedges, hitherto a bar to their formation, now proved a defence which the enemy could not pass. And when Bhagwán Dás had slain his most prominent adversary with his spear, and Akbar and the nephew had disposed of two others, the three took advantage of the momentary confusion of the enemy to charge forward, and aided by the desperate gallantry of their men, roused by the danger of their sovereign to extraordinary exertions, to force them to flight. The followers of the rebel chief, sensible that they were engaged in a losing cause, displayed nothing like the firmness and persistency of the soldiers of Akbar. They dropped off as they could find the opportunity, and the rebel chief himself, abandoned by his following, made his way, as best he could, past Ahmadábád and Dísa to Sirohí in Rájpútána.

Broach meanwhile had fallen, and there remained only Surat. Against this town, so well known to

English traders in the days of his son and grandson, Akbar marched in person on his return from the expedition just related. Against the breaching material employed in those days Surat was strong. But the Emperor pressed the siege with vigour, and after a patient progress of a month and seventeen days, the garrison, reduced to extremities, surrendered. He remained at Surat long enough to complete the settlement of the affairs of the province of Gujarát, and then began his return-march to Agra. He arrived there on the 4th of June, 1573, having been absent on the expedition about nine months.

Whilst Akbar had been besieging Surat, the rebel chief whom he had defeated at Sársa, and who had fled to Sirohí, had been bestirring himself to make mischief. Joined by another powerful malcontent noble he advanced against Pátan, met near that place the Emperor's forces, and had almost beaten them in the field, when, his own troops dispersing to plunder, the Mughal forces rallied, pierced the enemy's centre, and turned defeat into victory. The news of this achievement reached Akbar whilst he was still before Surat. The rebel leader, still bent on doing all the mischief in his power, made his way through Rájpútána to the Punjab, encountering two or three defeats on his way, but always escaping with his life, and plundering, as he marched, Pánípat, Sonpat, and Karnál. In the Punjab he was encountered by the imperial troops, was defeated, and, after some exciting adventures, was wounded by a party of fishermen near Múltán, taken prisoner, and died from the effect of his wound. He was a good riddance, for he was a masterful man. It may here be added that during this year the Mughal troops attempted, but failed to take the strong fortress of Kángra, in the Jálandhar Duáb. The besiegers had reduced the garrison to extremities when they were called off by the invasion of the adventurer whose death near Múltán I have recorded. Kángra did not fall to the Mughal till the reign of the son of Akbar.

Akbar had quitted the province of Gujarát believing that the conquest of the province was complete, and that he had won by his measures the confidence and affection of the people. But he had not counted sufficiently on the love of rule indwelling in the hearts of men who have once ruled: He had not been long at Agra, then, before the dispossessed lordlings of the province began to raise forces, and to harass the country. Determined to nip the evil in the bud, Akbar prepared a second expedition to Western India, and despatching his army in advance, set out, one Sunday morning in September, riding on a swift dromedary, to join it. Without drawing rein, he rode seventy miles to Toda, nearly midway between Jaipur and Ajmere. On the morning of the third day he reached Ajmere, paid his usual devotions at the tomb of the saint; then, mounting his horse in the evening, continued his journey, and joined his army at Páli on the road to Dísa. Near Pátan he was joined by some troops collected by his lieutenants, who had awaited the arrival of their sovereign to advance.

His force was small in comparison with that which the rebel chiefs had managed to enlist, but the men who formed it were the cream of his army. The celerity of his movements too had served him well. The rebels had not heard that he had quitted Agra when he was amongst them. They were in fact sleeping in their tents near Ahmadábád when Akbar, who had made the journey from Agra in nine days, was upon them.

That there was chivalry in those days is shown by the remark of the native historian, the author of the Tabakat-í-Akbarí, 'that the feeling ran through the royal ranks that it was unmanly to fall upon an enemy unawares, and that they would wait till he was roused.' The trumpeters, therefore, were ordered to sound. The chief rebel leader, whose spies had informed him that fourteen days before the Emperor was at Agra, still declared his belief that the horsemen before him could not belong to the royal army as there were no elephants with them. However he prepared for battle. The Emperor, still chivalrous, waited till he was ready, then dashed into and crossed the river, formed on the opposite bank, and 'charged the enemy like a fierce tiger.' Another body of Mughal troops took them simultaneously in flank. The shock was irresistible. The rebels were completely defeated, their leader wounded and taken prisoner.

An hour later, another hostile body, about five

thousand strong, appeared in sight. These too were disposed of, and their leader was killed. In the battle and in the pursuit the rebels lost about two thousand men. Akbar then advanced to Ahmadábád, rested there five days, engaged in rewarding the deserving, and in arranging for the permanent security of the province. He then marched to Mahmudábád, a town in the Kaira district, and thence to Sirohí. From Sirohí he went direct to Ajmere, visited there the mausoleum of the famous saint, thence, marching night and day, stopped at a village about fourteen miles from Jaipur to arrange with Rájá Todar Mall, whom he met there, one of the ablest of his officers, afterwards to become Diwán, or Chancellor, of the Empire, regarding the mode of levying the revenues of Gujarát. From that village the Emperor proceeded direct to Fatehpur-Síkrí, where he arrived in triumph, after an absence of forty-three days.

His plan of bringing under his sceptre the whole of India had so far matured that he ruled now, at the end of the eighteenth year of his reign, over Northwestern, Central, and Western India, inclusive of the Punjab and Kábul. Eastward, his authority extended to the banks of the Karamnásá. Beyond that river lay Behar and Bengal, independent, and under certain circumstances threatening danger. He had fully resolved, then, that unless the unforeseen should occur, the nineteenth year of his reign should be devoted to the conquest of Bengal and the states tributary to Bengal. Before setting out on the expedition, however, he paid another visit to the tomb of the saint on the hill of Ajmere.

I have written much in the more recent pages of the marches of Akbar, and the progress of his armies, but up to the present I have not referred to the principle on which those movements were made. There have been warriors, even within the memory of living men, who have made war support war. Upon that principle acted the Khorasání and Afghán barbarians who invaded India when the Mughal power was tottering to its fall. But that principle was not the principle of Akbar. Averse to war, except for the purpose of completing the edifice he was building, and which, but for such completion, would, he well knew, remain unstable, liable to be overthrown by the first storm, he took care that neither the owners nor the tillers of the soil should be injuriously affected by his own movements, or by the movements of his armies. With the object of carrying out this principle, he ordered that when a particular plot of ground was decided upon as an encampment, orderlies should be posted to protect the cultivated ground in its vicinity. He further appointed assessors whose duty it should be to examine the encamping ground after the army had left it, and to place the amount of any damage done against the government claim for revenue. The historian of the Tabakat-í-Akbarí adds that this practice became a rule in all his campaigns; 'and sometimes even bags of money were given to these inspectors, so that they might at once estimate and satisfy the claims of the raiyats and farmers, and obviate any interference with the revenue collectors.' This plan, which is in all essentials the plan of the western people who virtually succeeded to the Mughal, deprived war of its horrors for the people over whose territories it was necessary to march.

Whilst Akbar is paying a visit of twelve days' duration to the tomb of the saint at Ajmere, it is advisable that we examine for a moment the position of affairs in Behar and Bengal.

The Afghán king of Bengal and Behar, who sat upon the joint throne at the time of the Mughal re-conquest of the North-western Provinces, had after a time acknowledged upon paper the suzerainty of Akbar. But it was, and it had remained a mere paper acknowledgment. He had paid no tribute, and he had rendered no homage. During the second expedition of Akbar to Gujarát this prince had died. His son and immediate successor had been promptly murdered by his nobles, and these, constituting only a fraction, though a powerful fraction, of the court, had raised a younger brother, Dáúd Khán, to the throne. But Dáúd was a man who cared only for pleasure, and his accession was the cause of the revolt of a powerful nobleman of the Lodí family, who, raising his standard in the fort of Rohtásgarh, in the Shahábád district of Behar, declared his independence. A peace, however, was patched up between them, and Dáúd, taking advantage of this, and of the trust reposed in him by the Lodí nobleman, caused the latter to be seized and put to death. As soon as this intelligence reached the Mughal governor of Jaunpur, that nobleman, who had been directed by Akbar to keep a sharp eye on the affairs of Behar, and to act as circumstances might dictate, crossed the Karamnásá, and marched on the fortified city of Patná, into which Dáúd, distrustful of meeting the Mughals in the field, had thrown himself. Such was the situation very shortly after the return of Akbar from Gujarát. Desirous of directing the campaign himself, Akbar despatched orders to his lieutenant to suspend operations till he should arrive, then, making the hurried visit to Ajmere of which I have spoken, he hastened with a body of troops by water to Allahábád. Not halting there, he continued his journey, likewise by water, to Benares, stayed there three days, then, taking to boat again, reached the point where the Gúmtí flows into the Ganges. Thence, pending the receipt of news from his lieutenant, he resolved to ascend the Gúmtí to Jaunpur.

On his way thither, however, he received a despatch from his lieutenant, urging him to advance with all speed. Directing the boatmen to continue their course with the young princes and the ladies to Jaunpur, Akbar at once turned back, reached the point where he had left his troops, and directing that they should march along the banks in sight of the boats, descended to Chausá, the place memorable, the reader may recollect, for the defeat of his father by Sher Khán. Here a despatch reached him to the effect that the enemy had made a sortie from Patná, which had caused much damage to the besiegers. Akbar pushed on therefore, still by water, and reached the besieging army on the seventh day.

The next day he called a council of war. At this he expressed his opinion that before assaulting the fort it was advisable that the besiegers should occupy Hájípur, a town at the confluence of the Gandak and the Ganges, opposite to Patná. This course was adopted, and the next day Hájípur fell. Dáúd was so terrified by this success, and by the evident strength of the besieging army, that he evacuated Patná the same night, and fled across the Púnpún, near its junction with the Ganges at Fatwa. Akbar entered the city in triumph the next morning, but, anxious to capture Dáúd, remained there but four hours; then, leaving his lieutenant in command of the army, followed with a well-mounted detachment in pursuit of the enemy. Swimming the Púnpún on horseback he speedily came up with Dáúd's followers, and captured elephant after elephant, until on reaching Daryápur, he counted two hundred and sixty-five of those animals. Halting at Daryápur, he directed two of his trusted officers to continue the pursuit. These pressed on for fourteen miles further, then it became clear that Dáúd had evaded them, and they returned.

The conquest of Patná had given Behar to Akbar. He stayed then at Daryápur six days to constitute the government of the province, then nominating to the chief office the successful lieutenant who had planned the campaign, he left him to follow it up whilst he should return to Jaunpur. At that place he stayed thirty-three days, engaged in perfecting arrangements for the better administration of the country. With this view he brought Jaunpur, Benares, Chanar, and other mahalls in the vicinity, directly under the royal exchequer, and constituted the newly acquired territories south of the Karamnásá a separate government.

Having done this, he proceeded to Cawnpur, on his way to Agra. At Cawnpur he stayed four days, long enough to receive information that his general in Bengal had occupied, successively, Monghyr, Bhágalpur, Garhí, and Tanda on the opposite side of the Ganges to Gaur, the ancient and famous Hindu capital of Bengal, and that he was preparing to push on further. It may be added that he carried out this resolution with vigour, and followed up Dáúd relentlessly, defeating him at Bájhura, and finally compelling him to surrender at Cuttack. With the surrender of this prince, the conquest of Bengal might be regarded as achieved.

Very much elated with the good news received at Cawnpur, Akbar, deeming the campaign in Bengal virtually terminated, pushed on to Delhi, devoted there a few days to hunting, and then made another journey to Ajmere, hunting as he marched. At Nárnul he received visits from his governors of the Punjab and of Gujarát, and had the satisfaction of learning that everywhere his rule was taking root in the hearts of the people. After the exchange of ideas with these noblemen, he pushed on to Ajmere, made his pilgrimage to the tomb of the saint, caused to be repressed the rising of a petty chief in the jungles of Jodhpur, and then returned to his favourite residence at Fatehpur-Síkrí.

He had noticed, on his many journeys, that a very great part of the territories he had traversed remained uncultivated. The evil was neither to be attributed to the nature of the soil, which was rich, nor to the laziness of the people. Sifting the matter to the bottom, Akbar came to the conclusion that the fault rather lay with the administration, which placed upon the land a tax which rendered cultivation prohibitive to the poor man. The evil, he thought, might be remedied if some plan could be devised for dividing the profits of the first year between the government and the cultivator. After a thorough examination of the whole question, he arranged that the several parganás, or subdivisions of the districts, should be examined, and that those subdivisions which contained so much land as, on cultivation, would yield ten million of tankás[1], should be divided off, and given in charge of an honest and intelligent officer who was

[1] Blochmann, in his *Aín-i-Akbarí* (note, p. 16), states that, according to Abulfazl, the weight of one dam was five tanks. As the copper coin known as 'dam' was one fortieth part of a rupee (Ibid. p. 31), it follows that ten million of tankás would equal 50,000 rupees. A parganá is a division of land nearly equalling a barony. A parganadár was called 'lord of a barony.'

to receive the name of Karorí. The clerks and accountants of the exchequer were to make arrangements with these officers and send them to their respective districts, where, by vigilance and attention, the uncultivated land might in the course of three years be brought into a state of production, and the revenues recovered for the government. This scheme was carried out, and was found to realise all the advantages it promised.

The nineteenth year of the reign of Akbar was thus in all respects save one a glorious year for the young empire. Bengal and Behar had been added to North-western, Central, and Western India. Practically, in fact, all India north of the Vindhya range acknowledged the supremacy of the son of Humáyún. The exception to the general prosperity was caused by a terrible famine and pestilence in Western India, the effects of which were most severely felt. Grain rose to a fabulous price, 'and horses and cows had to feed upon the bark of trees.' The famine and pestilence lasted six months.

The early part of the following year, 1575, was occupied with the pursuit of Dáúd and the conquest of Orissa. I have already stated how the Afghán prince was defeated at Bájhura, midway between Mughalmárí and Jaleswar, and how, pursued to and invested in Cuttack, he had surrendered. The treaty concluded with him provided that he should govern the province of Orissa in the name and on behalf of the Emperor Akbar. It may be added that Dáúd did not keep the faith he plighted on this occasion. He took the first propitious occasion to rebel, and two years later was defeated in a great battle by the Mughal general. He was taken prisoner, and in punishment of his treason his head was severed from his body on the field of battle. For some time, however, Bengal and Orissa continued to require great vigilance and prompt action on the part of the Mughal administrators.

The other principal events of this year were the building by the Emperor at Fatehpur-Síkrí of an Ibádat-kháná, or palace for the reception of men of learning, genius, and solid acquirements. The building was divided into four halls: the western to be used by Saiyids, or descendants of the Prophet: the southern by the learned, men who had studied and acquired knowledge: the northern by those venerable for their wisdom and their subjection to inspiration. The eastern hall was devoted to the nobles and officers of state, whose tastes were in unison with those of one or other of the classes referred to. When the building was finished, the Emperor made it a practice to repair there every Friday night and on the nights of holy days, and spend the night in the society of the occupants of the halls, moving from one to the other and conversing. As a rule, the members of each hall used to present to him one of their number whom they considered most worthy of the notice and bounty of the Emperor. The visits were always made opportunities for the distribution of largesses, and scarcely one of the guests ever went empty away. The building was completed by the end of the year.

The following year was uneventful, but the year 1577 was marked by that rebellion in Orissa under Dáúd of which I have already spoken. The campaign was stirring whilst it lasted, but the death of Dáúd and his uncle put an end to it.

This year, likewise, there was trouble in Rájpútána. Alone of all the sovereigns of the territories known by that name, the Ráná of Mewár had refused the matrimonial alliance offered to his female relatives by Akbar. Descended, as he believed, from the immortal gods, he regarded such an alliance as a degradation. He refused it then, whilst he was yet struggling for existence. He refused it, though he saw the Rájpút prince whom he most hated, the Rájá of Jodhpur, enriched, in consequence of his compliance, by the acquisition of four districts, yielding an ample revenue. He remained obdurate, defying the power of Akbar. Ráná Udai Singh had in 1568 lost his capital, and had fled to the jungles of Rajpípla, and there had died in 1572.

His son, Partáp Singh, inherited all his obstinacy, and many of the noble qualities of his grandfather, the famous Sanga Ráná. Without a capital, without resources, his kindred and clansmen dispirited by the reverses of his house, yet sympathising with him in his refusal to ally himself with a Muhammadan, Partáp Singh had established himself at Kombalmír, in the Arávallis, and had endeavoured to organise the country for a renewed struggle. Some information of his plans seems to have reached the ears of Akbar whilst he was paying his annual visit to Ajmere in 1576-7, and he despatched his most trusted general, also a Rájpút, the Mán Singh of Jaipur, whom we have seen fighting by his side in Gujarát, with five thousand horse, to beat him up. The two opposing forces met at Huldíghát, called also Gogandah, in December 1576. The battle which followed terminated in the complete defeat of the Ráná, who, when the day was lost, fled to the Arávalli hills. To deprive him of all possible resources Akbar despatched a party into the hills, with instructions to lay waste the country whilst pursuing. Akbar himself entered Mewár, arranged the mode of its administration; then proceeded to Málwá, encamped on its western frontier, arranged the administration of the territories dependent upon the city of Burhánpur, and improved that of Gujarát. To these matters he devoted the years 1577-8. He then marched for the Punjab.

A circumstance, interesting to the people who now hold supreme sway in India, occurred to the Emperor on his way to the Punjab. He had reached Delhi, and had even proceeded a march beyond it, when a certain Hájí[1] who had visited Europe, 'brought with him fine goods and fabrics for his Majesty's inspection.' The chronicler does not state more on the subject than the extract I have made, and we are left to imagine the part of Europe whence the fabrics came, and the impression they made. Akbar stayed but a short time

[1] A Hájí is a Musalmán who has made the pilgrimage to Mekka.

in the Punjab, then returned to Delhi, paid then his annual visit to Ajmere, and stopping there but one night, rode, accompanied by but nine persons, at the rate of over a hundred miles a day to Fatehpur-Síkrí, arriving there the evening of the third day.

The following year, 1580, was remarkable for the fact that the empire attained the highest degree of prosperity up to that time. Bengal was not only tranquil, but furnished moneys to the imperial exchequer. The ruler of Mewár was still being hunted by the imperial troops, but in no other part of India was the sound of arms heard.

In the course of his journeys Akbar had noticed how the imposition of inland tolls, justifiable so long as the several provinces of Hindustán were governed by rival rulers, tended only, now that so many provinces were under one head, to perpetuate differences. Early in 1581, then, he abolished the tamgha, or inland tolls, throughout his dominions. The same edict proclaimed likewise the abolition of the jizyá, a capitation tax imposed by the Afghán rulers of India upon those subjects who did not follow the faith of Muhammad. It was the Emperor's noble intention that thought should be free; that every one of his subjects should worship after his own fashion and according to his own convictions, and he carried out this principle to the end of his days. The most important political event of the year was the rebellion of a body of disaffected nobles in Bengal. Acting without much cohesion they were defeated and dispersed.

The year following, 1582, Akbar marched at the head of an army to the Punjab to repulse an invasion made from Kábul by his own brother, Muhammad Hakím Mirzá. The rebel brother had arrived close to Lahore before Akbar had reached Pánípat. The news, however, of the march of Akbar produced upon him the conviction that his invasion must miscarry. He accordingly retreated from Lahore, and fell back on Kábul. Akbar followed him by way of Sirhind, Kálánaur, and Rotás; then crossed the Indus at the point where Attock now stands, giving, as he crossed the river, instructions for the erection of a fortress at that place.

He advanced on to Pesháwar, and pushed forward a division of his army under his son, Prince Murád, to recover Kábul. Murád was a young man, tall and thin, with a livid complexion, but much given to drink, from the effects of which he and his brother, Prince Dányál, eventually died. Marching very rapidly, he encountered the army of his uncle at Khurd-Kábul and totally defeated him. Akbar had followed him with a supporting army, and entered Kábul three days after him. There he remained three weeks, then, having pardoned his brother and rebestowed upon him the government of Kábul, he returned by way of the Khaibar to Lahore, settled the government of the Punjab, and then marched, by way of Delhi, to Fatehpur-Síkrí. 'He now,' writes the chronicler, 'remained for some time at Fatehpur, administering justice, dispensing charity, and arranging public business.'

Apparently he continued to reside there throughout the year following. Rebellion was still smouldering in Bengal, but the Emperor was represented there by capable officers who reported constantly to him, and to whom he as constantly despatched instructions. The disaffection was not very serious, but it was harassing and interfered greatly with the collection of the revenues.

The beginning of 1584 found Akbar still at Fatehpur-Síkrí. The principal events of the year were, the pacification of Bengal; the outbreak and suppression of a rebellion in Gujarát; the revolt of the ruler of Asírgarh and Burhánpur; disturbances in the Deccan; and the death of the brother of Akbar, the then ruler of Kábul. The revolts were put down and a new governor was sent to Kábul. Prosperity reigned over the empire when the year closed.

Among the firmest of the protected allies of the Emperor was Bhagwán Dás, Rájá of Jaipur, who had not only himself rendered splendid military service to Akbar, but whose nephew, Mán Singh, held a very high command in his armies. At the period at which we have arrived this Rájpút prince was governor of the Punjab. From his family Akbar now selected a wife for his son, Prince Salím, afterwards the Emperor Jahángír. The marriage was celebrated at Fatehpur-Síkrí, with great ceremony and amid great rejoicings. Until this reign the Rájpút princes had scornfully rejected the idea of a matrimonial alliance with princes of the Muhammadan faith. But it was the desire of Akbar to weld: to carry into action the cardinal principle that differences of race and religion made no difference in the man. He had many prejudices to overcome, especially on the part of the Rájpút princes, and to the last he could not conquer the obstinate resistance of the Ráná of Mewár.

The others were more complaisant. They recognised in Akbar the founder of a set of principles such as had never been heard before in India. In his eyes merit was merit, whether evinced by a Hindu prince or by an Uzbek Musalmán. The race and creed of the meritorious man barred neither his employment in high positions nor his rise to honour. Hence, men like Bhagwán Dás, Mán Singh, Todar Mall, and others, found that they enjoyed a consideration under this Muhammadan sovereign far greater and wider-reaching than that which would have accrued to them as independent rulers of their ancestral dominions. They governed imperial provinces and commanded imperial armies. They were admitted to the closest councils of the prince whose main object was to obliterate all the dissensions and prejudices of the past, and, without diminishing the real power of the local princes who entered into his scheme, to weld together, to unite under one supreme head, without loss of dignity and self-respect to any one, the provinces till then disunited and hostile to one another.

One of the means which Akbar employed to this end was that of marriage between himself, his family, and the daughters of the indigenous princes. There was, he well knew, no such equaliser as marriage. The Rájpút princes could not fail to feel that their relationship to the heir to the throne, often to the throne itself, assured their position. When they reflected on the condition of Hindustán prior to his rule; how the Muhammadan conquests of the preceding five centuries had introduced strife and disorder without cohesion, and that this man, coming upon them as a boy, inexperienced and untried in the art of ruling, had introduced order and good government, toleration and justice, wherever he conquered; that he conquered only that he might introduce those principles; that he made no distinction between men on account of their diversity of race or of religious belief; they, apt to believe in the incarnation of the deity, must have recognised something more than ordinarily human, something approaching to the divine and beneficent, in the conduct of Akbar.

His toleration was so absolute, his trust, once given, so thorough, his principles so large and so generous, that, despite the prejudices of their birth, their religion, their surroundings, they yielded to the fascination. And when, in return, Akbar asked them to renounce one long-standing prejudice which went counter to the great principle which they recognised as the corner-stone of the new system, the prejudice which taught them to regard other men, because they were not Hindus, as impure and unclean, they all, with one marked exception, gave way. They recognised that a principle such as that was not to be limited; that their practical renunciation of that portion of their narrow creed which forbade marriages with those of a different race, could not but strengthen the system which was giving peace and prosperity to their country, honour and consideration to themselves.

It was in the beginning of the thirty-first year of his reign that Akbar heard of the death of his brother at Kábul, and that the frontier province of Badakshán had been overrun by the Uzbeks, who also threatened Kábul. The situation was grave, and such as, he concluded, imperatively required his own presence. Accordingly, in the middle of November, he set out with an army for the Punjab, reached the Sutlej at the end of the following month, and marched straight to Ráwal Pindí. Learning there that affairs at Kábul were likely to take a direction favourable to his interests, he marched to his new fort of Attock, despatched thence one force under Bhagwán Dás to conquer Kashmír, another to chastise the Balúchís, and a third to move against Swát. Of these three expeditions, the last met with disaster. The Yusufzais not only repulsed the first attack of the Mughals, but when reinforcements, sent by Akbar under his special favourite, Rájá Bírbal, joined the attacking party, they too were driven back with a loss of 8,000 men, amongst whom was the Rájá[1]. It was the

[1] Rájá Birbal was a Bráhman, a poet, and a skilful musician. He was noted for his liberality and his *bonhomie*. 'His short verses, bon mots, and jokes,' writes Blochmann (*Ain-i-Akbari*, p. 405) 'are still in the mouths of the people of Hindustán.'

severest defeat the Mughal troops had ever experienced. To repair it, the Emperor despatched his best commander, Rájá Todar Mall, supported by Rájá Mán Singh, of Jaipur. These generals manœuvred with great caution, supporting their advance by stockades, and eventually completely defeated the tribes in the Khaibar Pass.

Meanwhile, the expedition sent against Kashmír had been but a degree more successful. The commanders of it had reached the Pass of Shuliyas, and had found it blockaded by the Musalmán ruler of the country. They waited for supplies for some days, but the rain and snow came on, and before they could move there came the news of the defeat inflicted by the Yusufzais. This deprived them of what remained to them of nerve, and they hastened to make peace with the ruler of Kashmír, on the condition of his becoming a nominal tributary, and then returned to Akbar. The Emperor testified his sense of their want of enterprise by according to them a very cold reception, and forbidding them to appear at court. But the mind of Akbar could not long harbour resentment, and he soon forgave them.

Of the three expeditions, that against the Balúchís alone was immediately successful. These hardy warriors submitted without resistance to the Mughal Emperor. As soon as the efforts of Todar Mall and Mán Singh had opened the Khaibar Pass, Akbar appointed the latter, the nephew and heir to the Jaipur Rájá, to be Governor of Kábul, and sent him thither with a sufficient force, other troops being despatched to replace him in the Yusufzai country, and Peshawar being strongly occupied. Akbar had himself returned to Lahore. Thence he directed a second expedition against Kashmír. As this force approached the Passes, in the summer of 1587, a rebellion broke out against the actual ruler in Srínagar. The imperial force experienced then no difficulty in entering and conquering the country, which thus became a portion of the Mughal empire, and, in the reign of the successor of Akbar, the summer residence of the Mughal sovereigns of India. It may here be mentioned that to reach Jamrúd, at the entrance of the Khaibar Pass, Mán Singh had to fight and win another battle with the hill-tribes. He reached Kábul, however, and established there a stable administration. The Kábulis and the heads of the tribes, however, complained to Akbar that the rule of a Rájpút prince was not agreeable to them, whereupon Akbar translated Mán Singh in a similar capacity to Bengal, which just then especially required the rule of a strong hand, and replaced him at Kábul by a Musalmán. He announced at the same time his intention of paying a visit to that dependency.

First of all, he secured possession of Sind (1588); then, in the spring of the following year, set out for Kashmír. On reaching Bhímbar, he left there the ladies of his harem with Prince Murád, and rode express to Srínagar. He remained there, visiting the neighbourhood, till the rainy season set in, when he sent his harem to Rotas. They joined him subsequently at Attock on his way to Kábul. The Passes to that capital were open, all opposition on the part of the hill-tribes having ceased, so Akbar crossed the Indus at Attock, and had an easy journey thence to Kábul. He stayed there two months, visiting the gardens and places of interest. 'All the people, noble and simple, profited by his presence[1].' He was still at Kábul when news reached him of the death of Rájá Todar Mall (November 10, 1589). The same day another trusted Hindu friend, Rájá Bhagwán Dás of Jaipur, also died. Akbar made then new arrangements for the governments of Kábul, Gujarát, and Jaunpur, and returned towards Hindustán.

He had already, as I have stated, arranged for the government of Bengal. He reached Lahore on his home journey in the beginning of 1590. Whilst residing there, information reached him that his newly appointed Governor of Gujarát, the son of his favourite nurse, had engaged in hostilities with Káthíawár and Cutch. These hostilities eventuated in the addition of those two provinces to the Emperor's dominions, and in the suicide of the prince of Afghán descent, who had fomented all the disturbances in Western India[2]. The Emperor took advantage of his stay at Lahore to direct the more

[1] Elliot, vol. v. p. 458.
[2] Vide Blochmann's *Ain-i-Akbari*, p. 326.

complete pacification of Sind, affairs in which province had taken a disadvantageous turn. The perfect conquest of the province proved more difficult than had been anticipated. It required large reinforcements of troops, and the display of combined firmness and caution to effect the desired result. The campaign took two years, and, during that time, Kashmír had revolted.

The Emperor during those two years had had his head-quarters at Lahore. No sooner did he hear that the success in Sind was complete, than Akbar, who, expecting the event, had sent on the bulk of his forces towards Bhímbar, remaining himself hunting on the banks of the Chenáb, set out to rejoin his main body. On his way to it he learned that his advanced guard had forced one of the Passes, notwithstanding fierce opposition. This event decided the war, for the soldiers of the rebel chief, resenting his action, fell upon him during the night, killed him, and cut off his head, which they sent to Akbar. With the death of this man all opposition ceased, and Akbar, riding on to Srínagar, stayed there eight days, settling the administration, and then proceeded by way of the gorge of Baramula to Rotas, and thence to Lahore. There he received information that his lieutenant in Bengal, the Rájá Mán Singh, had definitively annexed the province of Orissa to the imperial dominions. He had despatched thence to Lahore a hundred and twenty elephants, captured in that province, as a present to the Emperor.

The attempt to bring into the imperial scheme the Deccan provinces south of the Vindhyan range, followed the next year, and continued for eight years later. On the whole it was successful. The strong places, Daulatábád, Kherwá, Násik, Asírgarh, and Ahmadnagar, opened their gates, after long sieges, to the imperial arms. And, although the territories dependent upon Ahmadnagar were not entirely subdued till 1637, the position acquired by Akbar gave him a preponderance which the Mughals retained for at least a century.

The campaign in Southern India was remarkable for three facts. The first was the dissensions of the generals sent from different parts of India to co-operate independently in the conquest, dissensions which necessitated, first, the despatch thither from Agra of the Emperor's confidant, Abulfazl, and afterwards, the journey thither of Akbar himself; secondly, the death, from excessive drinking, of the Emperor's son, Prince Murád, at Jálna; thirdly, the murder of Abulfazl, on his return to Agra, at the instigation of Prince Salím, the eldest surviving son of Akbar and his heir apparent.

Akbar had held his court for fourteen years at Lahore when, in 1598, the necessities of the position in Southern India forced him to march thither. He had compelled the surrender of Ahmadnagar and Asírgarh, when, nominating Prince Dányál to be governor in Khándesh and Perár, and Abulfazl to complete the conquest of the territories dependent upon Ahmadnagar, he marched in the spring of 1601 towards Agra.

The circumstances which required the presence of Akbar at Agra were of a very painful character. Prince Salím had from his earliest youth caused him the greatest anxiety. Nor had the anxiety been lessened as the boy approached manhood. Salím, better known to posterity as the Emperor Jahángir, was naturally cruel, and he appeared incapable of placing the smallest restraint on his passions. He hated Abulfazl, really because he was jealous of his influence with his father; avowedly because he regarded him as the leading spirit who had caused Akbar to diverge from the narrow doctrines of the bigoted Muhammadans. Akbar had hoped for a moment that the despatch of Abulfazl to Southern India would appease the resentment of his son, and when he decided to proceed thither himself he had nominated Salím as his successor, and had confided to him, with the title of Viceroy of Ajmere, the task of finishing the war with the Ráná of Mewár, which had broken out again. He had further studied his partialities by despatching the renowned Mán Singh, his relation by marriage, to assist him.

The two princes were already on their march towards Mewár when information reached them that a rebellion had broken out in Bengal, of which province Mán Singh was Viceroy. Mán Singh was therefore compelled to march at once to repress the outbreak. Left without a counsellor, and commanding a considerable force, Prince Salím resolved to take advantage of the absence of his father in the south to make a bold stroke for the crown. Renouncing, then, his march on Mewár, he hurried with his force to Agra, and when the commandant of the imperial fortress, loyal to his master, shut its gates in his face, hastened to Allahábád, occupied the fort, seized the provinces of Oudh and Behar, and assumed the title of King.

It was the news of these occurrences which drew Akbar from the Deccan. Attributing the action of Salím to the violence of a temper which had ever been impatient of control, he resolved rather to guide than to compel him. Accordingly he wrote him a letter, in which, assuring him of his continued love if he would only return to his allegiance, he warned him of the consequences of continued disobedience. When this letter reached Salím, Akbar was approaching Agra at the head of an army of warriors, few in number, but the chosen of the empire. Salím, then, recognising that his position was absolutely untenable, and that if he persisted it might cost him the succession, replied in the most submissive terms. His conduct, however, did not correspond to his words. Informed, somewhat later, that the bulk of the imperial army was still in the Deccan, he marched to Itáwa, levying troops as he proceeded, with the intention of waiting upon his father at the head of an imposing force. But Akbar was not deceived. He sent his son an order to choose one of two courses; either to come to Agra slightly attended, or to return to Allahábád.

Prince Salím chose the latter course, receiving the promise, it is believed, that he should receive the grant of Bengal and Orissa. At any rate, he did receive the grant of those provinces. We cannot say, at this time, how much Akbar was influenced in his course by the consciousness of the comparative weakness of his own position, by his dislike of having to fight his own son, or by his affection. Probably the three sentiments combined to give to the course he adopted a tinge of weakness. At any rate, he soon had reason to feel that his concessions to his rebellious son had produced no good effect. For Salím, whose memory was excellent, and whose hatred was insatiable, took the opportunity of the return of Abulfazl from the Deccan, but slightly attended, to instigate the Rájá of Orchhá to waylay and murder him [1].

The murder of his friend was a heavy blow to Akbar. Happily he never knew the share his son had in that atrocious deed. Believing that the Rájá of Orchhá was the sole culprit, he despatched a force against him. The guilty Rájá fled to the jungles, and succeeded in avoiding capture, until the death of Akbar rendered unnecessary his attempts to conceal himself. A reconciliation with Salím followed, and

[1] Prince Salím justifies, in his *Memoirs*, the murder on the ground that Abulfazl had been the chief instigator of Akbar in his religious aberrations, as he regarded them. To the last he treated the Rájá of Orchhá with the greatest consideration.

the Emperor once more despatched his eldest son to put down the disturbances in Mewár. These disturbances, it may be mentioned, were caused by the continued refusal of Ráná Partáp Singh to submit to the Mughal. After his defeat at Huldíghát in 1576, that prince had fled to the jungles, closely followed by the imperial army. Fortune continued so adverse to him that after a series of reverses, unrelieved by one success, he resolved, with his family and trusting friends, to abandon Mewár, and found another kingdom on the Indus. He had already set out, when the unexampled devotion of his minister placed in his hands the means of continuing the contest, and he determined to try one more campaign. Turning upon his adversaries, rendered careless by continued success, he smote them in the hinder part, and, in 1586, had recovered all Mewár, the fortress of Chitor and Mandalgarh excepted. Cut off from Chitor, he had established a new capital at Udaipur, a place which subsequently gave its name to his principality. When he died, in 1597, he was still holding his own. He was succeeded by his son, Amra Ráná, who, at the time at which we have arrived, was bidding defiance, in Mewár, to all the efforts of the imperial troops (1603).

Prince Salím had a great opportunity. The forces placed at his disposal were considerable enough, if energetically employed, to complete the conquest of Mewár, but he displayed so little taste for the task that Akbar recalled him and sent him to his semi-independent government of Allahábád, where he spent his time in congenial debauchery, and in worse. His disregard of all sense of duty and honour, even of the lives of his most faithful attendants, became at last so marked that Akbar set out for Allahábád, in the hope that his presence might produce some effect. He had made but two marches, however, when the news of the serious illness of his own mother compelled him to return. But the fact that he had quitted Agra for such a purpose produced a revulsion in the thought and actions of Prince Salím. As his father could not come to him, he determined to repair, slightly attended, to the court of his father. There he made his submission, but he did not mend his ways, and his disputes with his eldest son, Prince Khusrú, became the scandal of the court.

The Emperor, indeed, was not happy in his children. His two eldest, twins, had died in infancy. The third, erroneously styled the first, was Prince Salím. The fate of the fourth son, Prince Murád, has been told. The fifth son, Prince Dányál, described as tall, well-built, good-looking, fond of horses and elephants, and clever in composing Hindustání poems, was addicted to the same vice as his brother Murád, and died about this time from the same cause. His death was a great blow to Akbar, who had done all in his power to wean his son from his excesses, and had even obtained a promise that he would renounce them. There were at court many grandsons of the Emperor. Of these the best-beloved was Prince Khurram, who subsequently succeeded Jahángír under the title of Sháh Jahán.

The news of the death of Prince Dányál and its cause seem to have greatly affected the Emperor. He was ill at the time, and it soon became evident that his illness could have but one termination. The minds of those about him turned at once to the consideration of the succession. His only surviving son was Prince Salím, but his conduct at Allahábád, at Agra, and elsewhere, had turned the hearts of the majority against him, whilst in his son, Prince Khusrú, the nobles recognised a prince whose reputation was untarnished. Prince Khusrú, moreover, as the son of a princess of Jodhpur, was closely related to Rájá Mán Singh, and that capable man was a great factor in the empire. He had married, too, the daughter of the Muhammadan nobleman who held the highest rank in the army, and who was himself probably related to the royal family, for he was the son of the favourite nurse of Akbar. These two great nobles began then to take measures for the exclusion of Prince Salím, and the succession of Prince Khusrú.

To effect this purpose they had the fort of Agra, in the palace in which Akbar was lying ill, guarded by their troops. Had Akbar died at this moment his death must have given rise to a civil war, for Salím would not renounce his pretensions. But, as soon as the prince recognised the combination against him, alarmed for his personal safety, he withdrew a short distance from Agra. Vexed at his absence during what he well knew was his last illness, Akbar, a lover above all of legality, summoned his nobles around him, declared Prince Salím to be his lawful successor, and expressed a hope that Prince Khusrú might be provided for by the government of Bengal.

The influence acquired by Akbar was never more apparent than at this conjuncture. It needed but one expression of resentment against his ungrateful and undutiful son to secure his exclusion. His expressions in his favour, on the other hand, had the effect of inducing the most powerful nobles to resolve to carry out his wishes, the half-hearted and wavering to join with them. Not even the highest nobleman in the army, the father-in-law of Prince Khusrú, who had already combined with Rájá Mán Singh to support Khusrú, could resist the influence. He sent privately to Prince Salím to assure him of his support. Mán Singh, the most influential of all at that particular crisis, seeing that he was isolated, yielded to the overtures made him by Salím, and promised also to uphold him. Secure now of the succession, Prince Salím repaired to the palace, where he was affectionately received by the dying Akbar. The circumstances of that interview are known only from the report of the prince.

After the first affectionate greetings Akbar desired that all the nobles might be summoned to the presence; 'for,' he added, 'I cannot bear that any misunderstanding should subsist between you and those who have for so many years shared in my toils, and been the companions of my glory.' When the nobles entered and had made their salutations, he said a few words to them in a body; then, looking at each of them in succession, he begged them to forgive him if he had wronged any one of them. Prince Salím then threw himself at his feet, weeping; but Akbar, signing to his attendants to gird his son with his own scimitar and to invest him with the turban and robes of State, commended to his care the ladies of the palace, urged him to be kind and considerate to his old friends and associates, then, bowing his head, he died.

Thus peacefully departed the real founder of the Mughal empire. More fortunate than his father and his grandfather, more far-sighted, more original, and, it must be added, possessing greater opportunities, he had lived long enough to convince the diverse races of Hindustán that their safety, their practical independence, their enjoyment of the religion and the customs of their forefathers, depended upon their recognition of the paramount authority which could secure to them these inestimable blessings. To them he was a man above prejudices. To all alike, whether Uzbek, or Afghán, or Hindu, or Pársí, or Christian, he offered careers, provided only that they were faithful, intelligent, true to themselves. The several races recognised that during his reign of forty-nine years India was free from foreign invasion; that he subjugated all adversaries within, some by force of arms, some by means more peaceful, and that he preferred the latter method. 'The whole length and breadth of the land,' wrote Muhammad Amín after his death. 'was firmly and righteously governed. All people of every description and station came to his court, and universal peace being established among all classes, men of every sect dwelt secure under his protection.' Such was Akbar the ruler. In the next chapter I shall endeavour to describe what he was as a man.

Akbar died the 15th October, 1605, one day after he had attained the age of sixty-three.

CHAPTER XII

THE PRINCIPLES AND INTERNAL ADMINISTRATION OF AKBAR

'THE success of the three branches of the government, and the fulfilment of the wishes of the subject,' writes the author of the Aín-í-Akbarí, ' whether great or small, depend upon the manner in which a king spends his time.'

Tried by this test, the cause of the success of Akbar as a man and as a ruler can be logically traced. Not only was he methodical, but there ran through his method a most earnest desire to think and do what was right in itself and conducive to the great aim of his life, the building of an edifice which, rooted in the people's hearts, would be independent of the personality of the ruler. Before I attempt to state in detail the means he adopted to attain this end, I propose to say a few words on a subject which may be said to underlie the whole question, the conformation of his mind and the manner in which it was affected by matters relating to the spiritual condition of mankind. Than this there cannot be any more important investigation, for it depended entirely on the structure of his mind, and its power to accept without prejudice, and judge impartially, views differing from those of his co-religionists, whether the chief of the Muhammadans, few in number when compared with the entire community, could so obtain the confidence and sympathy of the subject race, doomed to eternal perdition in the thought of all bigoted Musalmáns, as to overcome their prejudices to an extent which, had they been consulted previously, they would have declared impossible. The period was undoubtedly unfavourable to the development of what may be called a liberal policy in this matter.

The Muhammadans were not only conquerors, but conquerors who had spread their religion by the sword. The scorn and contempt with which the more zealous among them regarded the religion of the Hindus and those who professed it may be traced in every page of the writings of Badauní, one of the contemporary historians of the period. Nor was that scorn confined solely to the Hindu religion. It extended to every other form of worship and to every other doctrine save that professed by the followers of Muhammad.

Akbar was born in that creed. But he was born with an inquiring mind, a mind that took nothing for granted. During the years of his training he enjoyed many opportunities of noting the good qualities, the fidelity, the devotion, often the nobility of soul, of those Hindu princes, whom his courtiers, because they were followers of Bráhma, devoted mentally to eternal torments. He noted that these men, and men who thought like them, constituted the vast majority of his subjects. He noted, further, of many of them, and those the most trustworthy, that though they had apparently much to gain from a worldly point of view by embracing the religion of the court, they held fast to their own. His reflective mind, therefore, was unwilling from the outset to accept the theory that because he, the conqueror, the ruler, happened to be born a Muhammadan, therefore Muhammadanism was true for all mankind. Gradually his thoughts found words in the utterance: 'Why should I claim to guide men before I myself am guided;' and, as he listened to other doctrines and other creeds, his honest doubts became confirmed, and, noting daily the bitter narrowness of sectarianism, no matter of what form of religion, he became more and more wedded to the principle of toleration for all.

The change did not come all at once. The historian, Badauní, a bigoted Musalmán, who deplored what he considered the backsliding of the great sovereign, wrote: 'From his earliest childhood to his manhood, and from his manhood to old age, his Majesty has passed through the most various phases, and through all sorts of religious practices and sectarian beliefs, and has collected everything which people can find in books, with a talent of selection peculiar to him and a spirit of inquiry opposed to every (Islamite) principle. Thus a faith based on some elementary principles traced itself on the mirror of his heart, and as the result of all the influences which were brought to bear on his Majesty, there grew, gradually as the outline on a stone, the conviction on his heart that there were sensible men in all religions, and abstemious thinkers, and men endowed with miraculous powers, among all nations. If some true knowledge were thus everywhere to be found, why should truth be confined to one religion, or to a creed like Islám, which was comparatively new, and scarcely a thousand years old; why should one sect assert what another denies, and why should one claim a preference without having superiority conferred upon itself?'

Badauní goes on to state that Akbar conferred with Bráhmans and Sumánís, and under their influence accepted the doctrine of the transmigration of souls. There can be no doubt, however, but that the two brothers, Faizí and Abulfazl, like himself born and brought up in the faith of Islám, greatly influenced the direction of his studies on religion. It is necessary to say something regarding two men so illustrious and so influential. They were the sons of a Shaikh of Arab descent, Shaikh Mubárak, whose ancestors settled at Nagar, in Rájpútána. Shaikh Mubárak, a man who had studied the religion of his ancestors to the acquiring of a complete knowledge of every phase of it, who possessed an inquiring mind and a comprehensive genius, and who had progressed in thought as he acquired knowledge, gave his children an education which, grafted on minds apt to receive and to retain knowledge, qualified them to shine in any society. The elder son,

Shaikh Faizí, was born near Agra to the vicinity of which the father had migrated in 1547. He was thus five years younger than Akbar. Shortly after that prince had reconquered the North-western Provinces, Shaikh Faizí, then about twenty, began his quiet, unostentatious life of literature and medicine. He soon made a name as a poet. His native generosity, backed by the earnings of his profession as physician, prompted him to many acts of charity, and it became a practice with him to treat the poor for nothing.

In religious matters he, following his father's example, displayed a tendency towards the unfashionable doctrines of the Shiahs. It is related that, on one occasion, when he applied to the Kadr [1] for the grant of a small tract of land, that officer, who was a Sunní, not only refused him but, solely because he was a Shiah, drove him from the hall with contumely and insult. Meanwhile, moved by the report of his great ability, Akbar had summoned Faizí to his camp before Chitor, which place he was besieging. Faizí's enemies, and he had many, especially among the orthodox or Sunní Muhammadans, interpreted this order as a summons to be judged, and they warned the Governor of Agra to see that Faizí did not escape. But Faizí had no thought of escape. He was nevertheless taken to the camp of Akbar as a prisoner. The great prince received him with courtesy, and entranced by his varied talent,

---

[1] Kadr: an officer appointed to examine petitions, and selected on account of his presumed impartiality. Vide Blochmann's *Ain-i-Akbari*, p. 268.

shortly afterwards attached him to his court, as teacher in the higher branches of knowledge to the princes, his sons. He was occasionally also employed as ambassador.

His abundant leisure Faizí devoted to poetry. In his thirty-third year he was nominated to an office equivalent to that of Poet Laureate. Seven years later he died, never having lost the favour of Akbar, who delighted in his society and revelled in his conversation. It is said that he composed a hundred and one books. His fine library, consisting of four thousand three hundred choice manuscripts, was embodied in the imperial library.

But if Shaikh Faizí stood high in the favour of Akbar, his brother, Shaikh Abulfazl, the author of the Ain-í-Akbarí, stood still higher. Abulfazl was born near Agra the 14th January, 1551. He too, equally with his brother, profited from the broad and comprehensive teaching of the father. Nor did he fail to notice, and in his mind to resent, the ostracism and more than ostracism, to which his father was subjected on account of the opinions to which the free workings of a capacious mind forced him to incline. The effect on the boy's mind was to inculcate the value of toleration for all beliefs, whilst the pressure of circumstances stimulated him to unusual exertions in his studies. At the age of fifteen he had read works on all branches of those sciences that are based on reason and traditional testimony, and before he was twenty had begun his career as a teacher.

'An incident,' writes the lamented Professor Blochmann, ' is related to shew how extensive even at that time his reading was. A manuscript of the rare work of Içfahání happened to fall into his hands. Unfortunately, however, one half of each page, vertically downwards from top to bottom, was rendered illegible, or was altogether destroyed, by fire. Abulfazl, determined to restore so rare a book, cut away the burnt portions, pasted new paper to each page, and then commenced to restore the missing halves of each line, in which attempt, after many thoughtful perusals, he succeeded. Some time afterwards, a complete copy of the same work turned up, and on comparison it was found that in many places there were indeed different words, and in a few passages new proofs even had been adduced: but on the whole the restored portion presented so many points of extraordinary coincidence, that his friends were not a little astonished at the thoroughness with which Abulfazl had worked himself into the style and mode of thinking of a difficult author.'

A student by nature, Abulfazl for some time gave no favourable response to the invitation sent to him by Akbar to attend the imperial court. But the friendship which, in the manner already described, had grown between his elder brother, Faizí, and the Emperor, prepared the way for the intimacy which Akbar longed for, and when, in the beginning of 1574, Abulfazl was presented as the brother of Faizí, Akbar accorded to him a reception so favourable that he was induced to reconsider his resolve to lead a life 'of proud retirement.' He was then only twenty-three, but he had exhausted the sources of knowledge available in his own country. To use his own words: 'My mind had no rest, and my heart felt itself drawn to the sages of Mongolia or to the hermits on Lebanon; I longed for interviews with the Llámás of Tibet or with the pádris of Portugal, and I would gladly sit with the priests of the Pársís and the learned of the Zend-ávestá. I was sick of the learned of my own land.'

From this period he was attached to the court, and there arose between himself and Akbar one of those pure friendships founded on mutual esteem and mutual sympathy, which form the delight of existence. In the Emperor Abulfazl found the aptest of pupils. Amid the joys of the chase, the cares of governing, the fatigues of war, Akbar had no recreation to be compared to the pleasure of listening to the discussions between his much regarded friend and the bigoted Muhammadan doctors of law and religion who strove to confute him. These discourses constituted a great event in his reign. It is impossible to understand the character of Akbar without referring to them somewhat minutely. Akbar did not suddenly imbibe those principles of toleration and of equal government for all, the enforcement of which marks an important era in the history of India. For the first twenty years of his reign he had to conquer to maintain his power. With the representatives of dispossessed dynasties in Bengal, in Behar, in Orissa, in

Western India, including Gujarát and Khándesh, ready to seize an opportunity, to sit still was to invite attack. He was forced to go forward. The experience of the past, and the events daily coming under his notice, alike proved that there must be but one paramount authority in India, if India was to enjoy the blessings of internal peace.

During those twenty years he had had many intervals of leisure which he had employed in discussing with those about him the problem of founding a system of government which should retain by the sympathy of the people all that was being conquered. He had convinced his own mind that the old methods were obsolete; that to hold India by maintaining standing armies in the several provinces, and to take no account of the feelings, the traditions, the longings, the aspirations, of the children of the soil,—of all the races in the world the most inclined to poetry and sentiment, and attached by the strongest ties that can appeal to mankind to the traditions of their fathers— would be impossible.

That system, tried for more than four centuries, had invariably broken down, if not in the hands of the promulgator of it, certainly in those of a near successor. Yet none of those who had gone before him had attempted any other. His illustrious grandfather, who had some glimmering of the necessity, had not been allotted the necessary time, for he too had had to conquer to remain. His father had more than almost any of the Afghán sovereigns who preceded him failed to read the riddle. He fell before a better general, and his rootless system died at once, leaving not a trace behind it. Penetrated, then, with the necessity of founding a system that should endure, and recognising very gradually, that such a system must be based on mutual respect, on mutual toleration regarding differences of race, of religion, of tradition; on the union of interests; on the making it absolutely clear that the fall of the keystone to the arch meant the fall of each stone which went to build up the arch; he sought, as I have said, during the first twenty years of his reign, discussions with his courtiers and the learned regarding the system which would best appeal to those sentiments in the conquered race which would convey to them confidence and conviction.

Before Akbar knew Abulfazl he had almost withdrawn from the task in despair. Instead of wise counsel he encountered only precepts tending to bigotry and intolerance. From his earlier counsellors there was absolutely no help to be hoped for. Akbar became wearied of the squabbles of these men; of their leanings to persecution for the cause of religious differences, even amongst Muhammadans. Before even he had recognised the broad charity of the teachings of Abulfazl he had come to the conclusion that before founding a system of government it would be necessary to wage war against the bigoted professors who formed a power in his own empire. 'Impressed,' writes Professor Blochmann, 'with a favourable idea of the value of his Hindu subjects, he had resolved when pensively sitting in the evenings on the solitary stone at Fatehpur-Síkrí, to rule with an even hand all men in his dominions; but as the extreme views of the learned and the lawyers continually urged him to persecute instead of to heal, he instituted discussions, because, believing himself to be in error, he thought it his duty as ruler to "inquire."' These discussions took place every Thursday night in the Ibádat-Khána, a building at Fatehpur-Síkrí, erected for the purpose.

For a time Abulfazl took but a subordinate part in the discussions, simply spurring the various Muhammadan sectaries to reply to and demolish each other's arguments. The bigotry, the narrowness, evinced by the leaders of these sectaries, who agreeing that it was right to persecute Hindus and other unbelievers, hurled charges of infidelity against each other, quite disgusted Akbar. Instead of 'unity' in the creed of Islám he found a multiplicity of divisions. He was further disgusted with the rudeness towards each other displayed by the several sectaries, some of them holding high office in the State, and he was compelled on one occasion to warn them that any one of them who should so offend in the future would have to quit the hall. At last, one memorable Thursday evening, Abulfazl brought matters to a crisis. Foreseeing the opposition it would evoke, he proposed as a subject for discussion that a king should be regarded not only as the temporal, but as the spiritual guide of his subjects.

This doctrine struck at the fundamental principle of Islám, according to which the Kurán stands above every human ordinance. The point of Abulfazl's proposition lay in the fact that in preceding discussions the Muhammadan learned had differed not only regarding the interpretation of various passages of the Kurán, but regarding the moral character of Muhammad himself. The storm raised by Abulfazl's motion was, therefore, terrible. There was not a doctor or lawyer present who did not recognise that the motion attacked the vital principle of Islám, whilst the more clear-sighted and dispassionate recognised that the assertions made in their previous discussions had broken through 'the strong embankments of the clearest law and the most excellent faith.'

But how were they to resist a motion which affected the authority of Akbar? In this difficulty they came to a decision, which, though they called it a compromise, gave away in fact the whole question. They drew up a document[1] in which the Emperor was certified to be a just ruler, and as such was assigned the rank of a 'Mujtáhid,' that is, an infallible authority in all matters relating to Islám. This admission really conceded the object aimed at by Abulfazl, for, under its provisions, the 'intellect of the just king became the sole source of legislation,

[1] Blochmann (*Ain-i-Akbari*, p. xiv) calls it 'a document which I believe stands unique in the whole Church history of Islám.' He gives a copy of it at p. 186 of the same remarkable book.

and the whole body of doctors and lawyers bound themselves to abide by Akbar's decrees in religious matters.'

'The document,' writes Abulfazl in the Akbarnámah, 'brought about excellent results: (1) the Court became a gathering-place of the sages and learned of all creeds; the good doctrines of all religious systems were recognised, and their defects were not allowed to obscure their good features; (2) perfect toleration, or peace with all, was established; and (3) the perverse and evil-minded were covered with shame on seeing the disinterested motives of his Majesty, and thus stood in the pillory of disgrace.' It has to be admitted that two of the Muhammadan sectaries who had been the leaders of the party which inclined to persecution, signed the document most unwillingly, but sign they did. Abulfazl's father, on the other hand, who had exhausted all the intricacies of the creed of Islám, and the dogmas of its several sects, signed it willingly, adding to his signature that he had for years been anxiously looking forward to the realisation of the progressive movement.

The signature of this document was a turning-point in the life and reign of Akbar. For the first time he was free. He could give currency and force to his ideas of toleration and of respect for conscience. He could now bring the Hindu, the Pársí, the Christian, into his councils. He could attempt to put into execution the design he had long meditated of making the interests of the indigenous princes the interests of the central authority at Agra. The document is, in fact, the Magna Charta of his reign.

The reader will, I am sure, pardon me if I have dwelt at some length on the manner in which it was obtained, for it is the keystone to the subsequent legislation and action of the monarch, by it placed above the narrow restrictions of Islám. It made the fortune of Abulfazl. It gained for him, that is to say, the lasting friendship of Akbar. On the other hand it drew upon him the concentrated hatred of the bigots, and ultimately, in the manner related in the last chapter, caused his assassination.

One of the first uses made by Akbar of the power thus obtained was to clear the magisterial and judicial bench. His chief-justice, a bigoted Sunní, who had used his power to persecute Shiahs and all so-called heretics, including Faizí the brother of Abulfazl, was exiled, with all outward honour, to Mekka. Another high functionary, equally bigoted, received a similar mission, and the rule was inculcated upon all that in the eye of the law religious differences were to be disregarded, and that men, whether Sunnís, or Shiahs, Muhammadans or Hindus, were to be treated alike: in a word, that the religious element was not to enter into the question before the judge or magistrate.

From this time forth the two brothers, Faizí and Abulfazl, were the chief confidants of the Emperor in his schemes for the regeneration and consolidation of the empire. He caused them both to enter the military service, as the service which best secured their position at court. They generally accompanied him in his various expeditions, and whilst they suggested reforms in the land and revenue systems, they were at hand always to give advice and support to the views of the sovereign.

Meanwhile Akbar was preparing, in accordance with the genius of the age, and with the sentiments of the people over whom he ruled, to draw up and promulgate a religious code such as, he thought, would commend itself to the bulk of his people. The chief feature of this code, which he called Dín-í-Iláhí, or 'the Divine faith,' consisted in the acknowledgment of one God, and of Akbar as his Khalífah, or vicegerent on earth. The Islámite prayers were abolished as being too narrow and wanting in comprehension, and in their place were substituted prayers of a more general character, based on those of the Pársís, whilst the ceremonial was borrowed from the Hindus. The new era or date, which was introduced in all the government records, and also in the feasts observed by the Emperor, was exclusively Pársí. These observances excited little open opposition from the Muhammadans, but the bigoted and hot-headed amongst them did not the less feel hatred towards the man whom they considered the principal adviser of the sovereign. They displayed great jealousy, moreover, regarding the admission of Hindu princes and nobles to high commands in the army and influential places at court. It was little to them that these men, men like

Bhagwán Dás, Mán Singh, Todar Mall, Bírbal, were men of exceptional ability. They were Hindus, and, on that account and on that alone, the Muhammadan historians could not bring themselves to mention their names without sneering at their religion, and at the fate reserved for them in another world.

The inquiring nature of the mind of Akbar was displayed by the desire he expressed to learn something tangible regarding the religion of the Portuguese, then settled at Goa. He directed Faizí to have translated into Persian a correct version of the New Testament, and he persuaded a Jesuit priest, Padre Rodolpho Aquaviva, a missionary from Goa, to visit Agra.

It was on the occasion of the visit of this Father that a famous discussion on religion took place in the Ibádat-Khána, at which the most learned Muhammadan lawyers and doctors, Bráhmans, Jains, Buddhists, Hindu materialists, Christians, Jews, Zoroastrians or Pársís, each in turn spoke. The story is thus told by Abulfazl. 'Each one fearlessly brought forward his assertions and arguments, and the disputations and contentions were long and heated. Every sect, in its vanity and conceit, attacked and endeavoured to refute the statements of their antagonists. One night the Ibádat-Khána was brightened by the presence of Padre Rodolpho, who for intelligence and wisdom was unrivalled among Christian doctors. Several carping and bigoted men attacked him, and this afforded an opportunity for the display of the calm judgment and justice of the

L

assembly. These men brought forward the old received assertions, and did not attempt to arrive at truth by reasoning. Their statements were torn to pieces, and they were nearly put to shame, when they began to attack the contradictions of the Gospel, but they could not prove their assertions. With perfect calmness and earnest conviction of the truth the Padre replied to their arguments, and then he went on to say:

'"If these men have such an opinion of our Book, and if they believe the Kurán to be the true word of God, then let a furnace be lighted, and let me with the Gospel in my hand, and the 'Ulamá (learned doctors) with their holy book in their hands, walk into that testing-place of truth, and the right will be manifest." The black-hearted mean-spirited disputants shrank from this proposal, and answered only with angry words. This prejudice and violence greatly annoyed the impartial mind of the Emperor, and, with great discrimination and enlightenment, he said:

'"Man's outward profession and the mere letter of Muhammadanism, without a heartfelt conviction, can avail nothing. I have forced many Bráhmans, by fear of my power, to adopt the religion of my ancestors; but now that my mind has been enlightened with the beams of truth, I have become convinced that the dark clouds of conceit and the mist of self-opinion have gathered round you, and that not a step can be made in advance without the torch of proof. That course only can be beneficial which we select with clear judgment. To repeat the words of the creed, to perform circumcision, or to be prostrate on the ground from the dread of kingly power, can avail nothing in the sight of God:

Obedience is not in prostration on the earth:
Practice sincerity, for righteousness is not borne upon the brow!"'

Whatever we may think of this discussion, of the test of fire proposed by the Christian priest, we may at least welcome it as showing the complete toleration of discussion permitted at the Ibádat-Khána, and, above all, as indicating the tendency of the mind of Akbar. He had, in fact, reasoned himself out of belief in all dogmas and in all accepted creeds. Instead of those dogmas and those creeds he simply recognised the Almighty Maker of the world, and himself, the chiefest in authority in his world as the representative in it of God, to carry out his beneficent decrees of toleration, equal justice, and perfect liberty of conscience, so far as such liberty of conscience did not endanger the lives of others. He was very severe with the Muhammadans, because he recognised that the professors of the faith of the dominant party are always inclined to persecution. But he listened to all, and recognising in all the same pernicious feature, viz., the broad, generous, far-reaching, universal qualities attributed to the Almighty distorted in each case by an interested priesthood, he prostrated himself before the God of all, discarding the priesthood of all.

He has been called a Zoroastrian, because he recognised in the sun the sign of the presence of the Almighty. And there can be no doubt but that the simplicity of the system of the Pársís had a great attraction for him. In his own scheme there was no priesthood. Regarding himself as the representative in his world of the Almighty, he culled from each religion its best part, so as to make religion itself a helpful agency for all rather than an agency for the persecution of others. The broad spirit of his scheme was as much raised above the general comprehension of the people of his age, as were his broad political ideas. To bring round the world to his views it was necessary that 'an Amurath should succeed an Amurath.' That was and ever will be impossible. The result was that his political system gradually drifted after his death into the old narrow groove whence he had emancipated it, whilst his religious system perished with him. After the reigns of two successors, Muhammadan but indifferent, persecution once again asserted her sway to undo all the good the great and wise Akbar had effected, and to prepare, by the decadence of the vital principle of the dynasty, for the rule of a nation which should revive his immortal principle of justice to all and toleration for all.

In the foregoing remarks I have alluded to the fact that Akbar allowed liberty of conscience in so far as that liberty did not endanger the lives of others. He gave a marked example of this in his dealing with the Hindu rite of Satí. It is not necessary to explain that the English equivalent for the word 'Satí' is 'chaste or virtuous,' and that a Satí is a woman who burns herself on her husband's funeral pile. The custom had been so long prevalent among Hindu ladies of rank that not to comply with it had come to be regarded as a self-inflicted imputation on the chaste life of the widow. Still, the love of life is strong, and the widow, conscious of her own virtue, and unwilling to sacrifice herself to an idea, had occasionally shown a marked disinclination to consent to mount the pile. It had often happened then that the priests had applied to her a persuasion, either by threats of the terrors of the hereafter or the application of moral stimulants, to bring her to the proper pitch of willingness.

Such deeds were abhorrent to the merciful mind of Akbar, and he discouraged the practice by all the means in his power. His position towards the princes of Rájpútána, by whom the rite was held in the highest honour, would not allow him so far to contravene their time-honoured customs, which had attained all the force of a religious ordinance, to prohibit the self-sacrifice when the widow earnestly desired it. Before such a prohibition could be issued time must be allowed, he felt, for the permeation to the recesses of the palace of the liberal principles he was inaugurating. But he issued an order that, in the case of a widow showing the smallest disinclination to immolate herself, the sacrifice was not to be permitted.

Nor did he content himself with words only. Once, when in Ajmere, whilst his confidential agent, Jai Mall, nephew of Rájá Bihárí Mall of Ambar, was on a mission to the grandees of Bengal, news reached him that Jai Mall had died at Chausá. Jai Mall had been a great favourite with Akbar, for of all the Rájpútána nobles he had been the first to pay his respects to him, and had ever rendered him true and loyal service. He had married a daughter of Rájá Udai Singh of Jodhpur, a princess possessing great strength of will. When the news of her husband's death reached Ambar she positively refused to become a Satí. Under the orders of the Emperor she had an absolute right to use her discretion. But when she did use it to refuse, the outcry against her, headed by Udai Singh, her son, became so uncontrollable, that it was resolved to force her to the stake. Information of this reached Akbar, and he determined to prevent the outrage. He was just in time, for the pile was already lighted when his agents, one of them the uncle of the deceased, reached the ground, seized Udai Singh, dispersed the assembly, and saved the princess.

Attached as Akbar was to his learned and liberal-minded friends, Faizí and Abulfazl, he encouraged all who displayed a real love for learning, and a true desire to acquire knowledge. He hated pretence and hypocrisy. He soon recognised that these two qualities underlay the professions of the 'Ulamás (Muhammadan doctors of learning) at his court. When he had found them out, he was disgusted with them, and resolved to spare no means of showing up their pretensions.

'He never pardoned,' writes Professor Blochmann, 'pride and conceit in a man, and of all kinds of conceit, the conceit of learning was most hateful to him.' Hence the cry of the class affected by his action that he discouraged learning and learned men. He did nothing of the sort. There never has flourished in India a more generous encourager of the real thing. In this respect the present rulers of India might profit by his example. One of the men whose knowledge of history was the most extensive in that age, and who possessed great talents and a searching mind, was Khán-í-Ázam Mírzá, son of his favourite nurse. For a long time this man held fast to the orthodox profession of faith, ridiculing the 'new religion' of Akbar, and especially ridiculing Faizí and Abulfazl, to whom he applied nicknames expressing his sense of their pretensions. But at a later period he had occasion to make the pilgrimage to Mekka, and there he was so fleeced by the priests that his attachment to Islám insensibly cooled down. On his return to Agra, he became a member of the Divine Faith. He wrote poetry well, and was remarkable for the ease of his address and his intelligence. One of his many aphorisms has descended to posterity. It runs as follows : 'A man should marry four wives— a Persian woman to have somebody to talk to ; a Khorasání woman for his housework; a Hindu woman, for nursing his children ; and a woman from Marawánnáhr (Turkistan), to have some one to whip as a warning to the other three.'

One of the ablest warriors and most generous of men in the service of Akbar was Mírzá Abdurráhím, son of his old Atálik or preceptor, Bairám Khán. For many years he exercised the office of Khán Khánán, literally 'lord of lords,' tantamount to commander-in-chief. But he was as learned as he was able in the field. He translated the memoirs of Bábar, well described by Abulfazl as 'a code of practical wisdom,' written in Turkish, into the Persian language then prevalent at the court of Akbar, to whom he presented the copy. Amongst other writers, the historians, Nizám-u-dín Ahmad, author of the Tabákat-í-Akbarí, or records of the reign of Akbar; the authors of the Taríkhí-í-Alfí, or the history of Muhammadanism for a thousand years; and, above all, the orthodox historian, Abul Kádir Badauní, author of the Taríkh-í-Badauní, or Annals of Badauní, and editor and reviser of a history of Kashmír, stand conspicuous.

Badauní was a very remarkable man. Two years older than Akbar, he had studied from his early youth various sciences under the most renowned and pious men of his age, and had come to excel in music, history, and astronomy. His sweet voice procured for him the appointment of Court Imán for Fridays. For forty years Badauní lived at court in company with Shaikh Mubárik and his sons Faizí and Abulfazl, but there was no real friendship between them, as Badauní, an orthodox Musalmán, always regarded them as heretics. Under instructions from Akbar he translated the Rámáyana from its original Sanscrit into Persian, as well as part of the *Máhábhárata*. His historical work above referred to as the Taríkh-í-Badauní, and which is perhaps better known under its alternative title *Muntakhabat-ul-Tawarikh*, or *Selections from the Annals*, is especially valuable for the views it gives of the religious opinions of Akbar, and its sketches of the famous men of his reign.

Badauní died about eleven years before the Emperor, and his great work, the existence of which he had carefully concealed, did not appear until some time during the reign of Jahángír. It is a very favourite book with the bigoted Muhammadans who disliked the innovations of Akbar, and it continued to be more and more prized as those innovations gradually gave way to the revival of persecution for thought's sake.

It is perhaps unnecessary to give a record of the other learned men who contributed by their abilities, their industry, and their learning to the literary glory of the reign of Akbar. The immortal Ain contains a complete list of them, great and small. But, as concerning the encouragement given to arts and letters by the sovereign himself, it is fitting to add a few words. It would seem that Akbar paid great attention to the storing in his library of works obtained from outside his dominions, as well as of those Hindu originals and their translations which he was always either collecting or having rendered into Persian. Of this library the author of the Ain relates that it was divided into several parts. 'Some of the books are kept within, some without the Harem.

Each part of the library is subdivided, according to the value of the books and the estimation in which the sciences are held of which the books treat. Prose books, poetical works, Hindí, Persian, Greek, Kashmirian, Arabic, are all separately placed. In this order they are also inspected. Experienced people bring them daily, and read them before his Majesty, who hears every book from the beginning to the end. At whatever page the readers daily stop, his Majesty makes with his own pen a mark, according to the number of the pages; and rewards the readers with presents of cash, either in gold or silver, according to the number of leaves read out by them. Among books of renown there are few which are not read in his Majesty's assembly hall; and there are no historical facts of past ages, or curiosities of science, or interesting points of philosophy, with which his Majesty, a leader of impartial sages, is unacquainted.' Then follows a long list of books specially affected by the sovereign, some of which have been referred to in preceding pages.

I have, I think, stated enough to show the influence exercised by literary men and literature on the history of this reign. The influence, especially of the two learned brothers, Faizí and Abulfazl, dominated as long as they lived. That of Abulfazl survived him, for the lessons he had taught only served to confirm the natural disposition of his master. The principles which the brothers loved were the principles congenial to the disposition of Akbar. They were the principles of the widest toleration of opinion; of justice to all, independently of caste and creed; of alleviating the burdens resting on the children of the soil; of the welding together of the interests of all classes of the community, of the Rájpút prince, proud of his ancient descent and inclined to regard the Muhammadan invader as an outcast and a stranger; of the Uzbek and Mughal noble, too apt to regard the country as his own by right of conquest, and its peoples as fit only to be his slaves; of the settlers of Afghán origin, who during four centuries had mingled with, and become a recognised part of the children of the soil;. of the indigenous inhabitants, always ready to be moved by kindness and good treatment.

There was one class it was impossible to conciliate: the Muhammadan princes whose families had ruled in India, and who aspired to rule in their turn; who, in Bengal, in Orissa, in Behar, and in many parts of Western India, still exercised authority and maintained large armies. These men, regarding their title as superior to that of Akbar, and not recognising the fact that whilst their predecessors had lived on the surface, Akbar was sending roots down deep into the soil, resisted his pretensions and defied his power. How he tried conciliation with these men, and how their own conduct compelled him to insist on their expulsion, has been told in the last chapter.

I propose now to relate how the broad principles natural to Akbar and confirmed by his association with Faizí and Abulfazl, affected the system of administration introduced by the reforming sovereign. In a previous page of this chapter I have quoted an expression of his own, to the effect that he had, at one time of his reign, forced Bráhmans to embrace Muhammadanism. This must have happened because Akbar states it, but of the forced conversions I have found no record. They must have taken place whilst he was still a minor, and whilst the chief authority was wielded by Bairám. From the moment of his assumption of power, that is, from the day on which he gave the till then all-powerful Bairám Khán permission to proceed to Mekka, he announced his intention, from which he never swerved, to employ Hindus and Muhammadans alike without distinction. In the seventh year of his reign, he being then in the twenty-first year of his life, Akbar abolished the practice, heretofore prevailing, by which the troops of the conqueror were permitted to forcibly sell or keep in slavery the wives, children, and dependants of the conquered. Whatever might be the delinquencies of an enemy, his children and the people belonging to him were, according to the proclamation of the sovereign, to be free to go as they pleased to their own houses, or to the houses of their relatives. No one, great or small, was to be made a slave. 'If the husband pursue an evil course,' argued the liberal-minded prince, 'what fault is it of the wife? And if the father rebel, how can the children be blamed?'

The same generous and far-seeing policy was pursued with unabated vigour in the reform of other abuses. The very next year, the eighth of his reign, the Emperor determined to abolish a tax, which, though extremely productive, inflicted, as he considered, a wrong on the consciences of his Hindu subjects. There are no people in the world more given to pilgrimages than are the Hindus. Their sacred shrines, each with its peculiar saint and its specific virtue, abound in every province of Hindustán. The journeys the pilgrims have to make are often long and tedious, their length being often proportioned to the value of the boon to be acquired. In these pilgrimages the Afghán predecessors of the Mughal had recognised a large and permanent source of revenue, and they had imposed, therefore, a tax on all pilgrims according to the ascertained or reputed means of each.

Abulfazl tells us that this tax was extremely prolific, amounting to millions of rupees annually. But it was felt as a great grievance. In the eyes of the Hindu a pilgrimage was often an inculcated duty, imposed upon him by his religion, or its interpreter, the Bráhman priest. Why, he argued, because he submitted his body to the greatest inconvenience, measuring his own length along the ground, possibly for hundreds of miles, should he be despoiled by the State? The feelings of his Hindu subjects on this point soon reached the ears of Akbar. It was submitted to him by those who saw in the tax only an easy source of revenue that the making of pilgrimages was a vain superstition which the Hindus would not forego, and therefore the payment being certain and continuous, it would be bad financial policy to abolish the tax. Akbar, admitting that it was a tax on the superstitions of the multitude, and that a Hindu might escape paying it by staying at home, yet argued that as the making of pilgrimages constituted a part of the Hindu religion, and was, in a sense, a Hindu form of rendering homage to the Almighty, it would be wrong to throw the smallest stumbling-block in the way of this manifestation of their submission to that which they regarded as a divine ordinance. He accordingly remitted the tax.

Similarly regarding the jizyá, or capitation tax imposed by Muhammadan sovereigns on those of another faith. This tax had been imposed in the early days of the Muhammadan conquest by the Afghán rulers of India. There was no tax which caused so much bitterness of feeling on the part of those who had to pay it: not one which gave so much opportunity to the display and exercise of human tyranny. The reason why the sovereigns before Akbar failed entirely to gain the sympathies of the children of the soil might be gathered from the history of the proceedings connected with this tax alone. 'When the collector of the Diwán,' writes the author of the Tarikh-í-Fíruz Sháhí, 'asks the Hindus to pay the tax, they should pay it with all humility and submission. And if the collector wishes to spit into their mouths, they should open their mouths without the slightest fear of contamination, so that the collector may do so.... The object of such humiliation and spitting into their mouths is to prove the obedience of infidel subjects under protection, and to promote the glory of the Islám, the true religion, and to show contempt for false religions.' That the officials who acted in the manner here described contravened the true spirit of Islám, I need not stop to argue. There is not a religion which has not suffered from the intemperate zeal of its bigoted supporters; and Muhammadanism has suffered at least as much as the others. But the extract proves the extent to which it was possible for the agents of an unusually enlightened prince to tyrannise over and to insult the conquered race in the name of a religion, whose true tenets they perverted by so acting.

Akbar recognised not only the inherent liability to this abuse in the collection of such a tax, but also the vicious character of the tax itself. The very word 'infidel' was hateful to him. 'Who is certain that he is right?' was his constant exclamation. Recognising good in all religions, he would impose no tax on the conscientious faith of any man. Early then, in the ninth year of his reign, and in the twenty-third of his life, three years, be it borne in mind, before he had come under the influence of either of the two illustrious brothers, Faizí and Abulfazl, he, prompted by his own sense of the eternal fitness of things, issued an edict abolishing the jizyá. Thenceforth all were equal in matters of faith before the one Eternal.

The dealings of Akbar with the Hindus were not confined to the abolition of taxes which pressed hardly on their religious opinions. He endeavoured, with as little show of authority as was possible, to remove restrictions which interfered with the well-being and happiness of the people. What he did regarding Satí I have already related. The kindred question of the re-marriage of a widow met with the greatest encouragement from him. He even went further, and issued an edict rendering such re-marriage lawful. In the same spirit he forbade marriages before the age of puberty, a custom deeply rooted amongst the Hindus, and carried on even at the present day, though theoretically condemned by the wisest among them. He prohibited likewise the slaughter of animals for sacrifice, and trials by ordeal. Nor was he less stringent with those of the faith in which he was born. His method with them took the form rather of example, of persuasion, of remonstrance, than a direct order.

He discouraged the excessive practice of prayers, of fasts, of alms, of pilgrimages, but he did not forbid them. These were matters for individual taste, but Akbar knew well that in the majority of instances open professions were merely cloaks for hypocrisy; that there were many ways in which a man's life could be utilised other than by putting on an austere appearance, and making long prayers. The rite of circumcision could not, indeed, be forbidden to the Muhammadans, but Akbar directed that the ceremony should not be performed until the lad had attained the age of twelve. To humour the prejudices of the Hindus, he discouraged the slaughter of kine. On the other hand, he pronounced the killing and partaking of the flesh of swine to be lawful. Dogs had been looked upon by Muhammadans as unclean animals, and the strict Muhammadan of the present day still regards them as such. Akbar declared them to be clean. Wine is prohibited to the Muslim. Akbar encouraged a moderate use of it.

In the later years of his reign (1592) he introduced, to the great annoyance of the bigoted party at his court, the practice of shaving the beard. In a hot country such as India the advantages arising from the use of the razor are too obvious to need discussion. But, although the order was not obligatory, the compliance or non-compliance with the custom became a distinguishing mark at the imperial court. Few things are more repugnant to a devout Musalmán than the shaving of his beard. It was so then, and it is so now. The example set in this respect by the sovereign caused then many murmurs and much secret discontent.

Amongst others of the natural characteristics of Akbar may be mentioned his attachment to his relatives. Of one of these, a foster-brother, who persistently offended him, he said, whilst inflicting upon him the lightest of punishments: 'Between me and Azíz is a river of milk, which I cannot cross.' The spirit of these words animated him in all his actions towards those connected with him. Unless they were irreclaimable, or had steeped their hands in the blood

M

of others, he ever sought to win them back by his gentleness and liberality. He loved forgiving, reinstating, trusting, and though the exercise of these noble qualities led sometimes to his being imposed upon, they told in the long run. He was a good son, a loving husband, and perhaps too affectionate a father.

His sons suffered from the misfortune of having been born in the purple. One of them, Prince Dányál, was a prince of the highest promise, but the temptations by which he was surrounded, unchecked by his tutors, brought him to an early grave. Similarly with Prince Murád. As to his successor, Jahángír, he was, in most respects, the very opposite of his father. Towards the close of the reign he set an example which became a rule of the Mughal dynasty, that of trying to establish himself in the lifetime of his father, whose dearest friend, Abulfazl, he had caused to be assassinated. Nothing could exceed the exemplary patience and forbearance with which Akbar treated his unworthy son. Again, Akbar abhorred cruelty: he regarded the performance of his duty as equivalent to an act of worship to the Creator.

In this respect he made no difference between great and small matters. He was not content to direct that such and such an ordinance should be issued. He watched its working; developed it more fully, if it were successful; and marked the details of its action on the several races who constituted his subjects. He had much confidence in his own judgment of men. He was admittedly a good physiognomist. Abulfazl wrote of him that 'he sees through some men at a glance,' whilst even Badaúní admits the claim, though with his usual inclination to sneering at all matters bearing on the Hindus, he declares that Akbar obtained the gift of insight from the Jogís (Hindu ascetics or magicians).

With all his liberality and breadth of view Akbar himself was not free from superstition. He believed in lucky days. Mr. Blochmann states that he imbibed this belief from his study of the religion of Zoroaster, of which it forms a feature. His courtiers, especially those who were secretly opposed to his religious innovations, attributed his undoubted success to luck. Thus Badaúní writes of 'his Majesty's usual good luck overcoming all enemies,' whereas it was his remarkable attention to the carrying out of the details of laws and regulations which he and his councillors had thoroughly considered which ensured his success.

He was very fond of field sports, especially of hunting, but after the birth of the son who succeeded him he did not hunt on Fridays. If we can accept the authority of the Emperor Jahángír, Akbar had made a vow that he would for ever abstain from hunting on the sacred day if the mother of Jahángír should have a safe deliverance, and he kept it to the end of his life. There is abundant evidence to prove that Akbar was not only fond of music, but was very musical himself. He delighted in the old tunes of Khwárizm, and, according to Abulfazl, himself composed more than two hundred of these, 'which are the delight of young and old.' The same authority states that 'his Majesty had such a knowledge of the science of music as trained musicians do not possess.' Every day the court was treated to an abundance of music, the sounds of which have in all times been especially agreeable to Eastern monarchs. He also was gifted, to a considerable extent, with the genius of invention. The Ain records how he invented a carriage, a wheel for cleaning guns, and elephant gear; how, further, he made improvements in the clothing of his troops and in his artillery.

In his diet Akbar was simple, taking but one regular meal a day. He disliked meat, and abstained from it often for months at a time. He was specially fond of fruits, and made a study of their cultivation. Abulfazl records that he regarded fruits 'as one of the greatest gifts of the Creator,' and that the Emperor brought horticulturists of Irán and Turán to settle at Agra and Fatehpur-Síkrí. 'Melons and grapes have become very plentiful and excellent; and water-melons, peaches, almonds, pistachios, pomegranates, etc., are everywhere to be found.' He adds that fruits were largely imported from Kábul, Kandahár, Kashmír, Badakshán, and even from Samarkand. The Ain contains a long list of these, which the reader who knows India will read with pleasure. It is interesting to find that, even in those days, the first place among the sweet fruits of Hindustán is given to the mango. This fruit is described as 'unrivalled in colour, smell, and taste; and some of the gourmands of Turán and Irán place it above musk-melon and grapes.'

One word as to the daily habits of Akbar and to the manner in which he was accustomed to pass an ordinary day at Agra or Fatehpur-Síkrí. It would seem that he kept late hours, spending the evenings far into the early morning in conversation and discussion. In such matters he occupied himself, according to the record of Abulfazl, till 'about a watch before daybreak,' when musicians were introduced. At daybreak the sovereign retired into his private apartments, made his ablutions, dressed, and about an hour later presented himself to receive the homage of his courtiers. Then began the business of the day. Probably this was concluded often long before midday, when the one meal which Akbar allowed himself was usually served, though there was no fixed hour for it. The afternoon was the recognised hour of sleep. Sometimes Akbar devoted the early morning to field sports, and sometimes the late evenings to the game of chaugán, or polo, for which purpose balls made of the palás wood were used. The hottest hours of the day were the hours of rest and recuperation.

Akbar had not reigned long ere he recognised the importance of attaching to his throne the Hindu princes of Rájpútána by a tie closer even than that of mere friendship. It is interesting to note how he managed to overcome the inborn prejudices of the high caste princes of Rajast'hán to consent to a union which, in their hearts, the bulk of them regarded as a degradation. It would seem that his father, Humáyún, had to a certain extent prepared the way. In his erudite and fascinating work[1], Colonel Tod relates how Humáyún, in the earlier part of his reign, became the knight of the princess Kurnávatí of Chitor, and pledged himself to her service. That service he loyally performed. He addressed her always as 'dear and virtuous sister.' He also won the regard of Rájá Bihárí Mall of Amber, father of the Bhagwán Dás, so often mentioned in these pages.

Akbar subsequently married his daughter, and becoming thus connected with the House of Amber (Jaipur), could count upon Bhagwán Dás and his nephew and adopted son, Mán Singh, one of the greatest of all his commanders, as his firmest friends. Writing in another page of Bhagwán Dás, Colonel Tod describes him as 'the friend of Akbar, who saw the value of attaching such men to his throne.' He adds, and few men have ever enjoyed better opportunities of ascertaining the real feelings of the princes of Rájpútána, 'but the name of Bhagwán Dás is execrated as the first who sullied Rájpút purity by matrimonial alliance with the Islámite.' Prejudice is always strong, and nowhere stronger than in caste.

Rájpútána never produced greater or larger-minded princes than Bhagwán Dás and his nephew. Their intimate union with Akbar contributed more than any other circumstance to reconcile the Rájpúts to

---

[1] *Annals and Antiquities of Rajast'hán*, by Lieutenant-Colonel James Tod, second (Madras) edition, pp. 262, 282-3.

the predominance of the Mughal. The union was further cemented by the marriage, already referred to, between Prince Salím and a daughter of Bhagwán Dás. What the real influence of Akbar's administration was upon that chivalrous race may be gathered from the short summary which Colonel Tod, himself, more Rájpút in his sympathies than the Rájpúts themselves, devotes to his career.

'Akbar,' writes that author, 'was the real founder of the empire of the Mughals, the first successful conqueror of Rájpút independence. To this end his virtues were powerful auxiliaries, as by his skill in the analysis of the mind and its readiest stimulant to action, he was enabled to gild the chains with which he bound them. To these they became familiarised by habit, especially when the throne exerted its power in acts gratifying to national vanity, or even in ministering to the more ignoble passions.' Unable, apparently, to comprehend the principle which underlay the whole policy of Akbar, that of conquering that he might produce union, and regarding him as he rightly regarded his Afghán and Pathán predecessors, Colonel Tod attacks him for his conquests. Yet even Colonel Tod is forced to add: 'He finally succeeded in healing the wounds his ambition had inflicted, and received from millions that meed of praise which no other of his race ever obtained.' I need not add that if to render happiness to millions is one of the first objects of kingship, and if to obtain that end union has to be cemented by conquest, the means sanction the end. Akbar did not conquer in Rájpútána to rule in Rájpútána. He conquered that all the Rájpút princes, each in his own dominions, might enjoy that peace and prosperity which his predominance, never felt aggressively, secured for the whole empire.

From the Rájá of Jodhpur, Udai Singh, at the time the most powerful of the Rájpút princes, Akbar obtained the hand of his daughter for his son Salím. The princess became the mother of a son who succeeded his father as the Emperor Sháh Jahán. In him the Rájpút blood acquired a position theretofore unknown in India. Of this marriage, so happy in its results, Colonel Tod writes that Akbar obtained it by a bribe, the gift of four provinces which doubled the fisc of Márwár (Jodhpur). He adds: 'With such examples as Amber and Márwár, and with less power to resist temptation, the minor chiefs of Rajast'hán, with a brave and numerous vassalage, were transformed into satraps of Delhi, and the importance of most of them was increased by the change.' Truly did the Mughal historian designate them as 'at once the props and ornaments of the throne.'

There surely could not be a greater justification of the policy of Akbar with respect to Rájpútána and its princes than is contained in the testimony of this writer, all of whose sympathies were strongly with the Rájpúts.

Whilst on the subject of the imperial marriages, I may mention that Akbar had many wives, but of these eight only are authoritatively mentioned. His first wife was his cousin, a daughter of his uncle, Hindal Mirzá. She bore him no children, and survived him, living to the age of eighty-four. His second wife was also a cousin, being the daughter of a daughter of Bábar, who had married Mirzá Nuruddin Muhammad. She was a poetess, and wrote under the *nom de plume*, Makhfí (the concealed). His third wife was the daughter of Rájá Bihárí Mall and sister of Rájá Bhagwán Dás. He married her in 1560. The fourth wife was famed for her beauty: she had been previously married to Abdul Wásí. The fifth wife, mother of Jahángír, was a Jodhpur princess, Jodh Báei. As mother of the heir apparent, she held the first place in the harem. The sixth, seventh, and eighth wives were Muhammadans.

In the matter of domestic legislation Akbar paid considerable attention to the mode of collecting revenue. He found existing a system devised by Sher Sháh, the prince who had defeated and expelled his father. The principles upon which this system was based were (1) the correct measurement of the land; (2) the ascertaining the average production of a block of land per bíghá [1]; (3) the settlement of the proportion of that amount to be paid to the Government by each: (4) the fixing of the equivalent in money for the settled amount in kind. Akbar proposed rather to develope this principle than to interfere with it.

[1] A bíghá is a portion of land measuring in the North-west Provinces nearly five-eighths of an acre. In Bengal, it is not quite one-third of an acre.

With this object he established a uniform standard to supersede the differing standards theretofore employed.

'This laudable regulation,' we are told in the Ain, 'removed the rust of uncertainty from the minds of collectors, and relieved the subject from a variety of oppressions, whilst the income became larger, and the State flourished.' Akbar likewise caused to be adopted improved instruments of mensuration, and with these he made a new settlement of the lands capable of cultivation within the empire. We are told in the Ain that he was in the habit of taking from each bíghá of land ten sers (about twenty pounds) of grain as a royalty. This was at a later period commuted into a money payment. In each district he had storehouses erected to supply animals, the property of the State, with food; to furnish cultivators with grain for sowing purposes; to have at hand a provision in case of famine; and to feed the poor. These store-houses were placed in charge of men specially selected for their trustworthy qualities.

The land was in the earlier part of the reign divided into three classes according to its fertility, and the assessment was fixed on the average production of three bíghás, one from each division. The cultivator might, however, if dissatisfied with the average, insist on the valuation of his own crop. Five classifications of land were likewise made to ensure equality of payment in proportion to the quality of the land and its immunity from accidents, such as inundation. Other regulations were carefully formed to discriminate between the several varieties of soil, all having for their object the fixing of a system fair alike to the cultivator and the Government.

Gradually, as I have above indicated, as the Government became settled, a better principle was introduced to fix the amount payable to the State. For this purpose statements of prices for the nineteen years preceding the survey were called for from the village heads. From these an average was struck, and the produce was valued at the current rates. At first these settlements were annual, but as fresh annual rates were found vexatious, the settlement was made for ten years, on the basis of the average of the preceding ten.

To complete this agricultural system, Akbar made at the same time a new division of the country for revenue purposes. Under this scheme the country was marked out in parcels, each yielding a karór (ten millions) of *dáms*, equal to twenty-five thousand rupees. The collector of each of these parcels was called a karórí. Whenever a karórí had collected the sum of two lakhs of *dáms* [1], he was required to send it to the Treasurer-General at head-quarters. It was found, however, after a time, that the arbitrary division based simply upon a mathematical theory produced

---

[1] Two hundred thousand *dáms*, equivalent to five thousand rupees. A *dám* is a copper coin, the fortieth part of a rupee. The coin known as the *damri*, used at the present day for the purposes of calculation, is the eighth part of a *dám*.

confusion and disturbed ancient ways, of all others most congenial to the Hindus. After a trial, then, the artificial division was abandoned in favour of the ancient system of the people, under which the lands were parcelled out in conformity with the natural features of the country and the village system prevailing therein.

Against the farming of the revenue, as a certain mode of oppression, Akbar was very strong. He particularly enjoined upon his collectors to deal directly, as far as was possible, with the cultivator himself, rather than with the village headman. This was an innovation which, though based upon the best intentions, did not always answer. Custom counts for much in India, and custom pronounced in favour of the recognition of the influence of the chief man of the village, and it became necessary practically to deal, at least conjointly, with him.

When the Emperor took into consideration the circumstances attending the holding of lands, he found not only that grants had been made by his predecessors to unworthy objects, but that his own administrators had been guilty of bribery and corruption of various degrees. It was shortly after Faizí joined him in camp, and had acquired great influence with him, that his eyes were opened to these enormities. He found to his horror that the chief perpetrators of them were men who made the largest professions of sanctity. Then followed, almost immediately, the sarcastic exile of these men to Mekka:

then, a thorough inquiry into the department. There were four classes to whom it had been considered desirable that the sovereign should be able to render State assistance. The first class comprised the men who devoted themselves to literature and learning, and who had no means of their own. It had seemed desirable that such men should not be harassed by the need of having to care for their daily bread. The second class included those who 'toil and practise self-denial, and while engaged in the struggle with the selfish passions of human nature, have renounced the society of men.' The third, the weak and poor, who had no strength for toil. The fourth, honourable men of gentle birth, who, from want of knowledge, are unable to provide for themselves by taking up a trade.

To inquire into the circumstances of petitioners of these classes an experienced officer of presumably correct intentions had been appointed. He was entitled Sadr, or chief, and ranked above the Kází and the judges. When, in consequence of the inquiries set on foot at the instance of Faizí, it was discovered that the whole of this department was a hotbed of corruption, Akbar made a clean sweep of the officials, from the Sadr down to the smallest Kází, and nominated men drawn from a different class, fencing their functions with strict regulations.

But, as sovereign who had to reward great services rendered to the crown, Akbar required to dispose of large grants of land to men devoted to his service. Thus, he paid the Mansabdárs, or officers entrusted with high command, by temporary grants of land in lieu of a money allowance. He found that the most powerful of his immediate predecessors, the Sher Sháh who had expelled his father, Humáyún, had been more than lavish in his grants of land to his immediate followers, men mostly of Afghán descent. Akbar inquired into the circumstances under which these grants had been made, and in many instances he resumed them to bestow them upon his own adherents.

In acting in this way he only followed the precedent set him by previous sovereigns. But he had even more reason than that which precedent would sanction. He found that the land specified in the *firmán* granted to the holder but rarely corresponded in extent to the land which he actually held. Sometimes it happened that the language of the *firmán* was so ambiguously worded as to allow the holder to take all that he could get by bribing the Kázís and the provincial Sadr. Hence, in the interests of justice and the interests of the crown and the people, he had a perfect right to resume whatever, after due inquiry, he found to be superfluous. He discovered, moreover, that the 'Ulamá, or learned doctors, a class more resembling the pharisees of the New Testament than any class of which history makes record, and whom he cordially detested, had been very free in helping themselves during the period of his minority, and before the representations of Faizí had induced him to make inquiries. He therefore made the strictest investigation into their titles. When these were found faulty, or he had reason to believe that they had been dishonestly obtained, he resumed the grants, and exiled the ex-holders to Bukkur in Sind, or to Bengal, the climate of which had, in those days, a very sinister reputation. At the period of his reform, moreover, he greatly reduced the authority of the Sadr, transferring to his own hands the bulk of the power which had devolved upon them.

Regarding the general tendency and result of the reforms instituted by Akbar in the territorial system of the country, a distinguished writer[1] has recorded his judgment that, much as they 'promoted the happiness of the existing generation, they contained no principle of progressive improvement, and held out no hopes to the rural population by opening paths by which it might spread into other occupations, or rise by individual exertion within his own.' I venture, with some diffidence and with the greatest respect, to differ from this criticism. Akbar, admittedly, promoted the happiness of the generation amongst whom he lived. To have proceeded on the lines suggested by Mr. Elphinstone, he would have destroyed a principle which was then vital to the existence of Hindu society as it was constituted. Akbar went dangerously near to that point when he attempted to negotiate directly with the cultivators instead of through the headman of the village. He recognised in sufficient time that he must deal very charily and

[1] *The History of India*, by the Hon. Mountstuart Elphinstone.

cautiously with customs which had all the force of law, and he withdrew his order.

The chief adviser of Akbar in matters of revenue, finance, and currency was the Rájá Todar Mall, of whom I have spoken in the last chapter. He was a man of great ability and of tried integrity. Though attached to the court of a Muhammadan sovereign, he was an earnest Hindu, and performed faithfully all the ceremonies of his religion. On one occasion when accompanying Akbar to the Punjab, in the hurry of departure he forgot his idols. As he transacted no business before his daily worship he remained for several days without food or drink, and was at last with difficulty consoled by the Emperor.

Of the army the principal component force was cavalry. Elephants too constituted an important feature in the array of battle. As a rule the presence of elephants was supposed to indicate the presence of the Emperor, or rather, it was believed that the sovereign could not be present unless elephants were there. In the last chapter I have given an example of the happy mistake committed by a formidable antagonist of the Emperor in consequence of this prevailing impression.

The empire north of the Vindhyan range was portioned by the Emperor into twelve subahs or provinces. These were each governed by a viceroy, subordinate only to the sovereign. He held office during good behaviour, and was bound in all things to carry out the instructions of his master. Under him were local military officers called *fáujdárs*, who united in their own persons the duties devolving upon a chief of police and a military commander. To them was consigned the maintenance of peace in their several districts; the superintendence of military establishments within the same; the command of the regular troops there located; and, generally, the repression of disturbances.

The lines upon which justice was administered by the officers of Akbar were the same as those introduced by his Afghán predecessors. The Kurán was the basis upon which the law rested. But precedents often modified the strict interpretation. Where, moreover, the law leaned to severity it was again modified by the instructions drafted by the Emperor or his advisers. The leading features of these instructions were to temper justice with mercy. The high officers were enjoined to be sparing in capital punishments. In one rescript addressed to the Governor of distant Gujarát, that functionary was directed in no case, except in that of dangerous sedition, to inflict capital punishment until his proceedings had received the confirmation of the Emperor.

South of the Vindhyan range, in the division known as the Deccan, or South, the imperial possessions were originally divided into three subahs or commands. Subsequently, when new provinces and districts had been acquired, they were increased to six. After the death of Akbar these were all placed under one head, called the Subahdár, the precursor of the Nizám. With him, but subordinate to him, was associated an administrative financial officer called the Diwán, or Chancellor.

Akbar was a very magnificent sovereign. Though simple in his habits, he recognised, as the greatest of British Viceroys recognised after him, that show is a main element in the governing of an Eastern people. It is necessary to strike the eye, to let the subjects see the very majesty of power, the 'pomp and circumstance' attending the being whose nod indicates authority, who is to them the personified concentration on earth of the attributes of the Almighty. This is no mere idea. The very expressions used by the natives of India at the present day show how this thought runs through their imaginations. To them the man in authority, the supreme wielder of power, sits in the place of God. His *fiat* means to them weal or woe, happiness or misery. On days of ceremony, then, they expect that this all-powerful being shall display the ensigns of royalty, shall surround himself with the pomp and glitter which betoken state. Akbar thoroughly understood this and acted accordingly.

We are not left to the descriptions of the author of the Ain to realise the imposing grandeur of his ceremonies. The native historians speak of his five thousand elephants, his twelve thousand riding-horses, his camp-equipage containing splendid tents, comprising halls for public receptions, apartments for feasting, galleries for exercise, chambers for retirement, all of splendid material and rich and varied colours. They describe the Emperor himself on the days of special ceremonial seated in a rich tent, the awnings of which were thrown open, in the centre of carpeting of the softest material, covering at least two acres of ground, receiving the homage of his nobles. These occupied tents inferior only in degree to that of the sovereign. Then ensued, in the sight of the people, the ceremony of weighing the sovereign against various articles, to be distributed to those who needed them. According to the number of years the sovereign had lived there was given away an equal number of sheep, goats, and fowls to the breeders of those animals. A number of the smaller animals were likewise set at liberty. The Emperor himself distributed with his own hand almonds and fruits of the lighter sort among his courtiers.

On the great day of the festival Akbar seated himself on his throne, sparkling with diamonds, and surrounded by his chiefest nobles, all magnificently attired. Then there passed before him, in review, the elephants with their head and breast-plates adorned with rubies and other stones, the horses splendidly caparisoned, the rhinoceroses, the lions, the tigers, the panthers, the hunting-leopards, the hounds, the hawks, the procession concluding with the splendidly attired cavalry. This is no fancy picture. The like of it was witnessed by Hawkins, by Roe, and by Terry, in the time of the son and successor of Akbar, and those eminent travellers have painted in gorgeous colours the magnificence of the spectacle.

These scenes were witnessed only on days of high ceremony. At ordinary times Akbar was the simple, unaffected, earnest man, ever striving after truth, such as the work he accomplished gives evidence of. That work was the consolidation of an empire, torn by Muhammadan conquerors for more than four centuries, and at the end of that period still unsettled, still unconsolidated. During those four centuries the principles of the Kurán, read in a bigoted and unnatural sense by the Afghán conquerors, had been distorted to rob and plunder the Hindu population. The most enlightened of his earlier predecessors, Sultán Firuz Sháh, described by an English writer as possessing 'a humane and generous spirit,' confesses how he persecuted those who had not accepted the faith of Islám. Those principles of persecution for conscience sake, unchallenged at the time of the accession of Akbar, Akbar himself abolished.

Akbar's great idea was the union of all India under one head. A union of beliefs he recognised at a very early stage as impossible. The union therefore must be a union of interests. To accomplish such a union it was necessary, first, to conquer; secondly, to respect all consciences and all methods of worshipping the Almighty. To carry out this plan he availed himself to a modified extent only of the Muhammadan ritual. Instead of the formula under which so many persecutions had been organised, 'there is but one God, and Muhammad is his Prophet,' he adopted the revised version: 'there is but one God, and Akbar is his vicegerent on earth.' The prophet, he argued, came to preach the oneness, the unity, of God to an idolatrous people. To that people Muhammad was the messenger to proclaim the good tidings. But the precepts that messenger had laid down and had embodied in the Kurán had been interpreted to teach the propagation of the doctrine of the oneness of God by the sword.

The consequences of acting upon that mis-reading, as Akbar considered it, had been failure, at least in India. To that failure he had before him the witness of upwards of four centuries. He had but just entered his twenty-first year when he recognised that government carried on on such a principle must inevitably alienate. His object, I cannot too often repeat, was to bring together, to conciliate, to cement, to introduce a principle which should produce a community of interests among all his subjects. The germ of that principle he found in the alteration of the Musalmán profession of faith above stated. The writings of Muhammad, misinterpreted and misapplied, could only produce disunion. He, then, for his age and for his reign, would take the place of the Prophet. He would be the interpreter of the generous and merciful decrees of the one All-powerful.

The dominant religion should not be, as long as he was its interpreter, the religion of the sword. It should carry, on the contrary, a healing influence throughout India; should wipe away reminiscences of persecution, and proclaiming liberty of conscience, should practise the most perfect toleration. When this change had been generally recognised Akbar would then appeal to the princes and peoples of India to acknowledge the suzerainty of the one prince who would protect and yet not persecute. He would appeal to them to aid in the regeneration he was preparing, not in his individual interest, but in the interests of the millions who, for four centuries, had been harassed by invasions, by civil wars, by persecutions following both.

Akbar did not appeal to an unreflecting or an obstinate people. With one exception, that of Chitor (now known as Udaipur), the Rájpút princes and people of the most influential part of India came into his scheme. The most powerful amongst them, Jaipur and Jodhpur, helped him with the counsels of the men who, Hindus, were his most trusted captains, and with their splendid soldiers. The principal opposition he encountered was from the bigots of his own court, and from the descendants of the Afghán invaders settled in Bengal, in Orissa, and in Western India. For the sake of his beneficent scheme it was necessary to bring these into the fold. He tried at first to induce them to accept their authority from him. They accepted it only, on the first occasion, to seize an opportunity to rebel. There was then no choice but conquest. So he conquered. Toleration, good and equal laws, justice for all, invariably followed.

Thus it was that he, first of the Muhammadan invaders of India, welded together the conquered provinces, and made them, to the extent to which he conquered, for a portion of Southern India remained unsubdued, one united Empire. These are his titles to the admiration of posterity. We, who have watched his work, and have penetrated his motives, recognise the purity of his intentions. He did not wish, as the bigots of his Court declared that he wished, to have himself obeyed and worshipped as a God. No: he declared himself to be the interpreter of the religion of which the Prophet had been the messenger in the sense of teaching its higher truths, the truths of beneficence, of toleration, of equal justice irrespective of the belief of the conscience. His code was the grandest of codes for a ruler, for the founder of an empire.

'There is good in every creed; let us adopt what is good, and discard the remainder.' Such was his motto. He recognised this feature in the mild and benevolent working of Hinduism, in the care for the family inculcated by it, in the absence of the spirit of proselytism. He recognised it in the simple creed of the followers of Zoroaster. He recognised it in Christianity. There was good in all. He believed, likewise, that there was good in all men. Hence his great forbearance, his unwillingness to punish so long as there was hope of reform, his love of pardoning. 'Go and sin no more' was a precept that constituted the very essence of his conduct.

Such was Akbar, the founder of the Mughal dynasty. Such were the principles which enabled him to found it. They were principles which, if adhered to, would have maintained it. They were the principles by accepting which his Western successors maintain it at the present day.

In the foregoing pages I have spoken of Akbar and his achievements as though I were comparing him with the princes of our own day. Handicapped though he is by the two centuries which have since elapsed, Akbar can bear that comparison. Certainly, though his European contemporaries were the most eminent of their respective countries, though, whilst he was settling India, Queen Elizabeth ruled England, and Henry IV reigned in France, he need not shrink from comparison even with these. His reputation is built upon deeds which lived after him. No one can suppose that his successor, Jahángír, had he followed Humáyún, could have conciliated and welded together the divided territories he would have inherited or conquered. His passionate and bigoted character would have rendered the task impossible. But the foundations dug by Akbar were so deep that his son, although so unlike him, was able to maintain the empire which the principles of his father had welded together. When we reflect what he did, the age in which he did it, the method he introduced to accomplish it, we are bound to recognise in Akbar one of those illustrious men whom Providence sends, in the hour of a nation's trouble, to reconduct it into those paths of peace and toleration which alone can assure the happiness of millions.

INDEX

ABDUL MÁALÍ, favourite of Humáyún, is sent to occupy Dípálpúr, 62: rebellion, and death of, 97.

ABULFAZL, becomes the friend of Akbar, 151: character, studies, and influence of, 152-3, 170: murder of, 139.

AGRA, the building of the fort of, 99.

AGRICULTURE, measures taken by Akbar to benefit those addicted to, 121.

AKBAR, birth of, 52: is abandoned at Shál, 53: is taken to Kandahár, and tended by his aunt, 54: is removed to Kábul, 54, 55: where his father rejoins him, 55: perils of, at Kábul, 55-9: joins his father in the invasion of India, and is present at the battle of Sirhind, 62: is sent by his father to the Punjab, 63: is there proclaimed Emperor, 63: choice of courses before, 65: turns to contest the empire with Hemu, 66: moves on Pánípat, 68: wins the battle of Pánípat, 70: refuses to slay the captured Hemu, 71: the problem he had to solve in India, 78-80: personal appearance of, 81: character and predispositions of, 82-4: secures the Punjab, 84, 85: feels the preponderating influence of Bairám, 85-7: assumes the administration and exiles Bairám to Mekka, 88: suppresses the rebellion of Bairám, 89: personal rule of, begins, 91: the aims of, 92, 93: begins to carry out his plan of bringing all India into his system, 93: design of, of welding together, 94: deals with the Gakkhars, 96, 97: reception of, in Mándu, 98: deals with the revolt of the Uzbek nobles, 100: conquers Behar, 101, 102: suppresses rebellions in the Punjab and Kábul, 102: besieges Chitor, 105: founds Fatehpur-Sikrí, 106: after securing Rájpútána, marches on Gujarát, 108: incidents of the conquest of Gujarát by, 109-13: extent of the authority of, 115: reverses the principle of making war support war, 116: orders the invasion of Bengal, 118: and invades it himself, 118: captures Patná, 119: returns to Delhi, 120: and Fatehpur-Sikrí, 121: takes measures to benefit the agriculturists, 121: completes conquest of Bengal, 122: builds the Ibádat-kháná at Fatehpur-Sikrí, 123: abolishes inland tolls and the *jizyá*, 126: proceeds to Kábul, 127: reasons of, for matrimonial alliances with Rájput families, 129-31: proceedings of, in the

Punjab, 131-6: revisits Kábul, 134: proceeds to the Deccan, but returns to repress the rebellion of Prince Salím, 136-8: family of, 141: illness of, 142: dying words of, 144: character of, 144, 145: disposition, principles, and training of, 146: influence of Faizí over, 151: influence of Abulfazl over, 153-5: creed promulgated by, 157: uses made by, of his power, 159: religious code of, 160: culls from many religions, 161: his own conception of his position, 163: discourages Satí, 164: discourages professors, but encourages men of real learning, 166: his affection for Faizí and Abulfazl, 170: how the principles of, affected his administration, 171: making difference of religion no distinction, 172: abolishing the tax on pilgrimages, 172: the *jizyá*, 174: how they affected his dealings with the Hindus, 175: attachment of, to his relatives, 177: likings and peculiarities of, 179: fondness for field sports of, 179: daily habits of, 180: reasons of, for marriage with Rájput princesses, 181-4: wives of, 184: revenue system of, 185: rewards granted by, to the deserving, 189: wise caution displayed, by in disturbing ancient customs, 191: army of, 192: divisions of the empire of, 192: magnificence of, 194: a true seeker after truth, 197: character of the people he appealed to, 198: comparison of, with his European contemporaries, 200.

ÁLÍ KULÍ KHÁN-I-SHAIBÁNÍ, brilliantly captures Hemu's artillery, 68.

ARGUMENT, the, of the work, 5.

ATTOCK, on the Indus, built by Akbar, 127-31.

BÁBAR, family from which, was descended, 12: age of, at time of father's death, 13: loses Ferghána, 14: surprises Samarkand, 15: is defeated by the Uzbeks, 15: and flees to the deserts, 16: crosses the Oxus, and conquers Kábul, 18: impressions on the mind of, by first glance at the Punjab, 18: resolves to conquer Kandahár, 19: visits Herát, 19: terrible march of, from Herát to Kábul, 20: marches for Kandahár, 21: defeats his enemy and takes it, 22: vicissitudes of the fortunes of, against the Uzbeks, 23: is proclaimed ruler of Sind, 24: first, second, and third invasions of India by, 31: fourth invasion of India by, 32: fifth invasion of India by, 33: reaches Pánípat, 33: fights and wins the battle of Pánípat, 34: the position of, in India, 35: difficulties of, with his army, 37: generous and noble nature of, 39: methods of, to conquer the country, 39: defeats Sanga Ráná, 41: conquers large portions of Central India and of Oudh, 42: invades Behar, 43: health of, declines, 45: devotion of, to Humáyún, 46: dies, 46: character of, 47, 48: last words of, 48.

BAIRÁM KHÁN, the best general of Humáyún, invades Jálandhar, 62; defeats the generals of Sikandar Sháh on the Sutlej, and marches to Sirhind, 62; is joined by Humáyún and Akbar, and helps to defeat Sikandar Sháh, 62: goes with Akbar to the Punjab as his Atálik, 63; murders Tardí Beg, 67, 68; urges Akbar to slay the captured Hemu, 70, 71; virtually rules the new conquest, 85; is exiled to Mekka by order of Akbar, 88; rebels, is defeated, and assassinated, 89, 90.

BENGAL, king of, in the time of Akbar, 117: is invaded by Akbar, 118: submits to Akbar, 122: Mán Singh appointed Governor of, 133.
BHAGWÁN DÁS, of Jaipur, Rájá, connection of, with Akbar, 111: gallantry of, 111: is governor of the Punjab, 128: death of, 134.
BIRBAL, Rájá, is killed by the Yusufzais, 131, and note.
DÁNYÁL, Prince, the one failing of, causes death of, 141, 142.
DÁÚD KHÁN, king of Bengal, vide BENGAL.
DECCAN, the, campaigns in, and partial conquest of, 136.

FAIZÍ, Shaikh, story of, 150: how he influenced the actions of Akbar, 151, 170.
FATEHPUR-SIKRÍ, founded by Akbar, 106, 107: discussions in the Ibádat-khaná at, 123: memorable scenes at, 156, 157, 161.
FERGHÁNÁ, kingdom of, 13, 14.

GAKKHARS, the, are subdued by Akbar, 96, 97.
GUJARÁT, story of the conquest of, by Akbar, 108-15.

HEMU, rise to power of, 61: wins two victories and threatens Delhi, 62, 63: defeats Tardí Beg and occupies Delhi, 66: moves towards Pánípat, 68: is attacked, and defeated by Akbar, 70: is slain, 71.
HERÁT, position of, in the time of Bábar, 17: route between, and Kábul, 20: is conquered by the Uzbeks, 21.
HUMÁYÚN, eldest son of Bábar and father of Akbar, assists his father in the conquest of India, 40: is sent for at the time of his father's illness, 45: sickness, and recovery of, 46: succeeds Bábar, 50: character of, 50: after a reign of eight years is driven from India by Sher Sháh, 50, 51: spends two and a half years in Sind, 51: wooes, wins, and marries Hámidá Begam, 52, 53: flight of, to Amarkót, 52: action of, on learning of the birth of Akbar, 53: sets out for Kandahár, 53: is forced to abandon Akbar at Shál, 53: conquers Kandahár and Kábul, 55: vicissitudes of fortune between, and Kámrán, at Kábul, 55-9: resolves to recover India, 59: invades India, 61: defeats Sikandar Sháh at Sirhind, 62; death of, 63, 64.

INDIA, sketch of history of, before the Mughal invasion, 26: character of the rule of dynasties prior to that of the Mughal, 27, 30; Bábar's position in, after Pánípat, 35: internal condition of, at the time, 36: position of, at the time of the death of Bábar, 48: general condition of, in the middle of the 16th century, 72-80.

KÁBUL, kingdom of, in the time of Bábar, 17: Akbar is removed to, 54, 55: vicissitudes of fortune between Humáyún and Kámrán at, 55-9: Akbar appeases troubles at, 102: Akbar restores order at, 127.
KÁMRÁN, Mirzá, vicissitudes of fortune in contest of with Humáyún, 54-9: finally succumbs, 59.
KANDAHÁR, important position of, recognised by Bábar, 19: taken by Bábar, 22: is captured by the Uzbeks, 23: is secured by Bábar, 31: Akbar is taken to, 53, 54: is conquered by Humáyún, 55.
KASHMÍR, conquest of, by Akbar, 131-5.

KHUSRÚ, Prince, chances of, to succeed Akbar, 141-3.

LEARNED MEN, who flourished in the time of Akbar, notice of some of the, 166-9.

LIBRARY, the, of Akbar, 169.

MÁN SINGH, of Jaipur, gallantry of, in Gujarát, 111: appointed Governor of Kábul, 132: on the remonstrance of the Kábulis is transferred to Bengal, 133: conduct of, during Akbar's illness, 143.

MEWÁR, Ráná of, refuses to come into Akbar's system, 124: is defeated at Huldíghát, 125: still fights for his own hand, 140.

MURÁD, Prince, son of Akbar, death of, 136.

ORCHHÁ, the Rájá of, is prompted by Prince Salím to murder Abulfazl, 139, and note.

ORISSA, conquest of, by Akbar, 118-22.

PÁNÍPAT, the first battle of, 33, 34: second battle of, 68-71.

PATNÁ, taken by Akbar, 119.

PUNJAB, the Bábar's first impressions of, 18: renews his acquaintance with, 32: again, 33: Akbar enters, and pursues his enemy into the Siwáliks 63-6: sojourn of Akbar in, 131-6.

RÁJPÚTÁNA, matrimonial alliances of Akbar with the royal families of, 128, 181: dealings with the several princes of, 91-143.

SALÍM, Prince (afterwards the Emperor Jahángír), character of, 137: rebels, 138: causes the murder of Abulfazl, 139: vicious conduct of, 140-42: apparent repentance of, 144: is girt with his dying father's sword, 144.

SAMARKAND, city of, surprised by Bábar, 15: taken by the Uzbeks, 15: is reconquered by, and captured from, Bábar, 23.

SANGÁ, Ráná, position of, in Rájpútána, 40: is defeated by Bábar, 41.

SHAIBÁNÍ KHÁN, vide UZBEK.

SHER KHÁN, afterwards Sher Sháh, revolts from Bábar, 43: drives Humáyún from India, 50, 51: reign of, 60: defects of rule of, and predecessors of, 73-8.

SIKANDAR SHÁH, claims the rule over Muhammadan India, 61: is defeated by Humáyún at Sirhind, and flees to the Siwáliks, 62: again shows signs of life, 63: retreats into Mánkót, 65: pursued by Akbar, surrenders on terms, 84, 85.

SIND, Bábar is proclaimed ruler of, 24: completion of the conquest of, under Akbar, 134, 135.

TARDÍ BEG, prudent conduct of, on the death of Humáyún, 64: is defeated by Hemu, 66: joins Akbar at Sirhind. 67: where he is murdered by Bairám, 68.

TODAR MALL, Rájá, is sent by Akbar to repair the defeat of his troops by the Yusufzais, 132: death of, 134: influence of, with Akbar, 192.

UMERSHAIKH, father of Bábar, 13.

UZBEKS, the, defeat Bábar before Samarkand 15: conquer Herát, 21: take Kandahár, 23: contests of, with Bábar, 23: the, nobles, revolt against Akbar, 100: are forgiven, 101.

YUSUFZAIS, the, repulse the troops of Akbar, 131: are defeated by Todar Mall, 132.

THE END.

RULERS OF INDIA:

THE CLARENDON PRESS SERIES OF INDIAN HISTORICAL RETROSPECTS.

Edited by SIR W. W. HUNTER, K.C.S.I., M.A., LL.D.

The following 26 volumes have been published :—

I. *A BRIEF HISTORY OF THE INDIAN PEOPLES*, by SIR WILLIAM WILSON HUNTER, K.C.S.I. Twenty-first Edition; 82nd thousand. Price 3s. 6d.

II. *AKBAR: and the Rise of the Mughal Empire*, by COLONEL MALLESON, C.S.I., Author of *A History of the Indian Mutiny; The History of Afghanistan*. Fourth thousand. 2s. 6d.

III. *ALBUQUERQUE: and the Early Portuguese Settlements in India*, by H. MORSE STEPHENS, Esq., M.A., Balliol College, Lecturer on Indian History at Cambridge, Author of *The French Revolution; The Story of Portugal, &c.* 2s. 6d.

IV. *AURANGZÍB: and the Decay of the Mughal Empire*, by STANLEY LANE POOLE, Esq., B.A., Author of *The Coins of the Mughal Emperors; The Life of Stratford Canning; Catalogue of Indian Coins in the British Museum, &c.* 2s. 6d.

V. *MADHAVA RAO SINDHIA: and the Hindú Reconquest of India*, by H. G. KEENE, Esq., M.A., C.I.E., Author of *The Moghul Empire, &c.* 2s. 6d.

VI. *LORD CLIVE: and the Establishment of the English in India*, by COLONEL MALLESON, C.S.I. 2s. 6d.

VII. *DUPLEIX: and the Struggle for India by the European Nations*, by COLONEL MALLESON, C.S.I., Author of *The History of the French in India, &c.* Fourth thousand. 2s. 6d.

VIII. *WARREN HASTINGS:* and the Founding of the British Administration, by Captain L. J. Trotter, Author of *India under Victoria*, &c. Fourth thousand. 2s. 6d.

IX. *THE MARQUESS CORNWALLIS:* and the Consolidation of British Rule, by W. S. Seton-Karr, Esq., sometime Foreign Secretary to the Government of India, Author of *Selections from the Calcutta Gazettes*, 3 vols. (1784-1805). Third thousand. 2s. 6d.

X. *HAIDAR ALÍ AND TIPÚ SULTÁN:* and the Struggle with the Muhammadan Powers of the South, by Lewin Bentham Bowring, Esq., C.S.I., sometime Private Secretary to the Viceroy (Lord Canning) and Chief Commissioner of Mysore, Author of *Eastern Experiences*. 2s. 6d.

XI. *THE MARQUESS WELLESLEY:* and the Development of the Company into the Supreme Power in India, by the Rev. W. H. Hutton, M.A., Fellow and Tutor of St. John's College, Oxford. 2s. 6d.

XII. *THE MARQUESS OF HASTINGS:* and the Final Overthrow of the Maráthá Power, by Major Ross of Bladensburg, C.B., Coldstream Guards; F.R.G.S. 2s. 6d.

XIII. *MOUNTSTUART ELPHINSTONE:* and the Making of South-Western India, by J. S. Cotton, Esq., M.A., formerly Fellow of Queen's College, Oxford, Author of *The Decennial Statement of the Moral and Material Progress and Condition of India*, presented to Parliament (1885), &c. 2s. 6d.

XIV. *SIR THOMAS MUNRO:* and the British Settlement of the Madras Presidency, by John Bradshaw, Esq., M.A., LL.D., Inspector of Schools, Madras. 2s. 6d.

XV. *EARL AMHERST:* and the British Advance eastwards to Burma, chiefly from unpublished papers of the Amherst family, by Mrs. Anne Thackeray Ritchie, Author of *Old Kensington*, &c., and Richardson Evans, Esq. 2s. 6d.

RULERS OF INDIA SERIES.

XVI. *LORD WILLIAM BENTINCK:* and the Company as a Governing and Non-trading Power, by DEMETRIUS BOULGER, Esq., Author of *England and Russia in Central Asia; The History of China, &c.* 2s. 6d.

XVII. *EARL OF AUCKLAND:* and the First Afghan War, by CAPTAIN L. J. TROTTER, Author of *India under Victoria, &c.* 2s. 6d.

XVIII. *VISCOUNT HARDINGE:* and the Advance of the British Dominions into the Punjab, by his Son and Private Secretary, the Right Hon. VISCOUNT HARDINGE. Third thousand. 2s. 6d.

XIX. *RANJIT SINGH:* and the Sikh Barrier between our Growing Empire and Central Asia, by SIR LEPEL GRIFFIN, K.C.S.I., Author of *The Punjab Chiefs, &c.* Third thousand. 2s. 6d.

XX. *JOHN RUSSELL COLVIN:* the last Lieutenant-Governor of the North-Western Provinces under the Company, by his son, SIR AUCKLAND COLVIN, K.C.S.I., late Lieutenant-Governor of the North-Western Provinces. 2s. 6d.

XXI. *THE MARQUESS OF DALHOUSIE:* and the Final Development of the Company's Rule, by SIR WILLIAM WILSON HUNTER, K.C.S.I., M.A. Seventh thousand. 2s. 6d.

XXII. *CLYDE AND STRATHNAIRN:* and the Suppression of the Great Revolt, by MAJOR-GENERAL SIR OWEN TUDOR BURNE, K.C.S.I., sometime Military Secretary to the Commander-in-Chief in India. Fourth thousand. 2s. 6d.

XXIII. *EARL CANNING:* and the Transfer of India from the Company to the Crown, by SIR HENRY S. CUNNINGHAM, K.C.I.E., M.A., Author of *British India and its Rulers, &c.* Third thousand. 2s. 6d.

XXIV. *LORD LAWRENCE:* and the Reconstruction of India under the Crown, by SIR CHARLES UMPHERSTON AITCHISON, K.C.S.I., LL.D., formerly Foreign Secretary to the Government of India, and Lieutenant-Governor of the Punjab. Third thousand. 2s. 6d.

RULERS OF INDIA SERIES.

XXV. *THE EARL OF MAYO: and the Consolidation of the Queen's Rule in India*, by SIR WILLIAM WILSON HUNTER, K.C.S.I., M.A., LL.D. Third thousand. 2s. 6d.

SUPPLEMENTARY VOLUME.

XXVI. *JAMES THOMASON: and the British Settlement of North-Western India*, by SIR RICHARD TEMPLE, Bart., M.P., formerly Lieutenant-Governor of Bengal, and Governor of Bombay. Price 3s. 6d.

The Clarendon Press History of India, 3s. 6d.

A BRIEF HISTORY OF THE INDIAN PEOPLES.

STANDARD EDITION (TWENTY-FIRST), REVISED TO 1895.
EIGHTY-SECOND THOUSAND.

This Edition incorporates the suggestions received by the author from Directors of Public Instruction and other educational authorities in India; its statistics are brought down to the Census of 1891; and its narrative to 1892. The work has received the emphatic approval of the organ of the English School Boards, and has been translated into five languages. It is largely employed for educational purposes in Europe and America and as a text-book prescribed by the University of Calcutta for its Entrance Examination from 1886 to 1891.

'"A Brief History of the Indian Peoples," by W. W. Hunter, presents a sort of bird's-eye view both of India and of its people from the earliest dawn of historical records .... A work of authority and of original value.'—*The Daily News* (London).

'Dr. Hunter may be said to have presented a compact epitome of the results of his researches into the early history of India; a subject upon which his knowledge is at once exceptionally wide and exceedingly thorough.'—*The Scotsman.*

'Within the compass of some 250 pages we know of no history of the people of India so concise, so interesting, and so useful for educational purposes as this.'—*The School Board Chronicle* (London).

'For its size and subject there is not a better written or more trustworthy history in existence.'—*The Journal of Education.*

'So thoroughly revised as to entitle it to separate notice.'—*The Times.*

'Dr. Hunter's history, if brief, is comprehensive. It is a storehouse of facts marshalled in a masterly style; and presented, as history should be, without the slightest suspicion of prejudice or suggestion of partisanship. Dr. Hunter observes a style of severe simplicity, which is the secret of an impressive presentation of details.'—*The Daily Review* (Edinburgh).

'By far the best manual of Indian History that has hitherto been published, and quite equal to any of the Historical Series for Schools edited by Dr. Freeman. We trust that it will soon be read in all the schools in this Presidency.'—*The Times of India.*

Extract from a criticism by Edward Giles, Esq., Inspector of Schools, Northern Division, Bombay Presidency:—'What we require is a book which shall be accurate as to facts, but not overloaded with them; written in a style which shall interest, attract, and guide uncultivated readers; and short, because it must be sold at a reasonable price. These conditions have never, in my opinion, been realized previous to the introduction of this book.'

'The publication of the Hon. W. W. Hunter's "School History of India" is an event in literary history.'—*Reis & Rayyet* (Calcutta).

'He has succeeded in writing a history of India, not only in such a way that it will be read, but also in a way which we hope will lead young Englishmen and young natives of India to think more kindly of each other. The Calcutta University has done wisely in prescribing this brief history as a text-book for the Entrance Examination.'—*The Hindoo Patriot* (Calcutta).

o

Opinions of the Press
ON
SIR WILLIAM HUNTER'S 'DALHOUSIE.'

'An interesting and exceedingly readable volume..... Sir William Hunter has produced a valuable work about an important epoch in English history in India, and he has given us a pleasing insight into the character of a remarkable Englishman. The "Rulers of India" series, which he has initiated, thus makes a successful beginning in his hands with one who ranks among the greatest of the great names which will be associated with the subject.'—*The Times.*

'To no one is the credit for the improved condition of public intelligence [regarding India] more due than to Sir William Hunter. From the beginning of his career as an Indian Civilian he has devoted a rare literary faculty to the task of enlightening his countrymen on the subject of England's greatest dependency.... By inspiring a small army of fellow-labourers with his own spirit, by inducing them to conform to his own method, and shaping a huge agglomeration of facts into a lucid and intelligible system, Sir W. Hunter has brought India and its innumerable interests within the pale of achievable knowledge, and has given definite shape to the truths which its history establishes and the problems which it suggests.... Such contributions to literature are apt to be taken as a matter of course, because their highest merit is to conceal the labour, and skill, and knowledge involved in their production; but they raise the whole level of public intelligence, and generate an atmosphere in which the baleful influences of folly, ignorance, prejudice, and presumption dwindle and disappear.'—*Saturday Review.*

'Admirably calculated to impart in a concise and agreeable form a clear general outline of the history of our great Indian Empire.'—*Economist.*

'A skilful and most attractive picture.... The author has made good use of public and private documents, and has enjoyed the privilege of being aided by the deceased statesman's family. His little work is, consequently, a valuable contribution to modern history.'—*Academy.*

'The book should command a wide circle of readers, not only for its author's sake and that of its subject, but partly at least on account of the very attractive way in which it has been published at the moderate price of half-a-crown. But it is, of course, by its intrinsic merits alone that a work of this nature should be judged. And those merits are everywhere conspicuous.... A writer whose thorough mastery of all Indian subjects has been acquired by years of practical experience and patient research.'—*The Athenæum.*

'Never have we been so much impressed by the great literary abilities of Sir William Hunter as we have been by the perusal of "The Marquess of Dalhousie.".... The knowledge displayed by the writer of the motives of Lord Dalhousie's action, of the inner working of his mind, is so complete, that Lord Dalhousie himself, were he living, could not state them more clearly.... Sir William Hunter's style is so clear, his language so vivid, and yet so simple, conveying the impressions he wishes so perspicuously that they cannot but be understood, that the work must have a place in every library, in every home, we might say indeed every cottage.'—*Evening News.*

'Sir William Hunter has written an admirable little volume on "The Marquess of Dalhousie" for his series of the "Rulers of India." It can be read at a sitting, yet its references—expressed or implied—suggest the study and observation of half a life-time.'—*The Daily News.*

Opinions of the Press
ON
SIR WILLIAM HUNTER'S 'LORD MAYO.'

'Sir William W. Hunter has contributed a brief but admirable biography of the Earl of Mayo to the series entitled "Rulers of India," edited by himself (Oxford, at the Clarendon Press).'—*The Times.*

'In telling this story in the monograph before us, Sir William Hunter has combined his well-known literary skill with an earnest sympathy and fulness of knowledge which are worthy of all commendation.... The world is indebted to the author for a fit and attractive record of what was eminently a noble life.'—*The Academy.*

'The sketch of The Man is full of interest, drawn as it is with complete sympathy, understanding, and appreciation. But more valuable is the account of his administration. No one can show so well and clearly as Sir William Hunter does what the policy of Lord Mayo contributed to the making of the Indian Empire of to-day.'—*The Scotsman.*

'Sir William Hunter has given us a monograph in which there is a happy combination of the essay and the biography. We are presented with the main features of Lord Mayo's administration unencumbered with tedious details which would interest none but the most official of Anglo-Indians; while in the biography the man is brought before us, not analytically, but in a life-like portrait.'—*Vanity Fair.*

'The story of his life Sir W. W. Hunter tells in well-chosen language—clear, succinct, and manly. Sir W. W. Hunter is in sympathy with his subject, and does full justice to Mayo's strong, genuine nature. Without exaggeration and in a direct, unaffected style, as befits his theme, he brings the man and his work vividly before us.'—*The Glasgow Herald.*

'All the knowledge acquired by personal association, familiarity with administrative details of the Indian Government, and a strong grasp of the vast problems to be dealt with, is utilised in this presentation of Lord Mayo's personality and career. Sir W. Hunter, however, never overloads his pages, and the outlines of the sketch are clear and firm.' —*The Manchester Express.*

'This is another of the "Rulers of India" series, and it will be hard to beat.... Sir William Hunter's perception and expression are here at their very best.'—*The Pall Mall Gazette.*

'The latest addition to the "Rulers of India" series yields to none of its predecessors in attractiveness, vigour, and artistic portraiture.... The final chapter must either be copied verbally and literally—which the space at our disposal will not permit—or be left to the sorrowful perusal of the reader. The man is not to be envied who can read it with dry eyes.'—*Allen's Indian Mail.*

'The little volume which has just been brought out is a study of Lord Mayo's career by one who knew all about it and was in full sympathy with it.... Some of these chapters are full of spirit and fire. The closing passages, the picture of the Viceroy's assassination, cannot fail to make any reader hold his breath. We know what is going to happen, but we are thrilled as if we did not know it, and were still held in suspense. The event itself was so terribly tragic that any ordinary description might seem feeble and laggard. But in this volume we are made to feel as we must have felt if we had been on the spot and seen the murderer "fastened like a tiger" on the back of the Viceroy.'—*Daily News*, Leading Article.

Opinions of the Press

ON

MR. W. S. SETON-KARR'S 'CORNWALLIS.'

'This new volume of the "Rulers of India" series keeps up to the high standard set by the author of "The Marquess of Dalhousie." For dealing with the salient passages in Lord Cornwallis's Indian career no one could have been better qualified than the whilom foreign secretary to Lord Lawrence.'—*The Athenæum.*

'We hope that the volumes on the "Rulers of India" which are being published by the Clarendon Press are carefully read by a large section of the public. There is a dense wall of ignorance still standing between the average Englishman and the greatest dependency of the Crown; although we can scarcely hope to see it broken down altogether, some of these admirable biographies cannot fail to lower it a little. . . . Mr. Seton-Karr has succeeded in the task, and he has not only presented a large mass of information, but he has brought it together in an attractive form. . . . We strongly recommend the book to all who wish to enlarge the area of their knowledge with reference to India.'—*New York Herald.*

'We have already expressed our sense of the value and timeliness of the series of Indian historical retrospects now issuing, under the editorship of Sir W. W. Hunter, from the Clarendon Press. It is somewhat less than fair to say of Mr. Seton-Karr's monograph upon Cornwallis that it reaches the high standard of literary workmanship which that series has maintained.'—*The Literary World.*

MRS. THACKERAY RITCHIE'S AND MR. RICHARDSON EVANS'

'LORD AMHERST.'

'The story of the Burmese War, its causes and its issues, is re-told with excellent clearness and directness.'—*Saturday Review.*

'Perhaps the brightest volume in the valuable series to which it belongs. . . . The chapter on "The English in India in Lord Amherst's Governor-Generalship" should be studied by those who wish to understand how the country was governed in 1824.'—*Quarterly Review.*

'There are some charming pictures of social life, and the whole book is good reading, and is a record of patience, skill and daring. The public should read it, that it may be chary of destroying what has been so toilsomely and bravely acquired.'—*National Observer.*

'The book will be ranked among the best in the series, both on account of the literary skill shown in its composition and by reason of the exceptional interest of the material to which the authors have had access.'—*St. James's Gazette.*

Opinions of the Press
ON
MR. S. LANE-POOLE'S 'AURANGZÍB.'

'There is no period in Eastern history so full of sensation as the reign of Aurangzíb.... Mr. Lane-Poole tells this story admirably; indeed, it were difficult to imagine it better told.'—*National Observer.*

'Mr. Lane-Poole writes learnedly, lucidly, and vigorously.... He draws an extremely vivid picture of Aurangzíb, his strange ascetic character, his intrepid courage, his remorseless overthrow of his kinsmen, his brilliant court, and his disastrous policy; and he describes the gradual decline of the Mogul power from Akbar to Aurangzíb with genuine historical insight.'—*Times.*

'A well-knit and capable sketch of one of the most remarkable, perhaps the most interesting, of the Mogul Emperors.'—*Saturday Review.*

'As a study of the man himself, Mr. Lane-Poole's work is marked by a vigour and originality of thought which give it a very exceptional value among works on the subject.'—*Glasgow Herald.*

'The most popular and most picturesque account that has yet appeared... a picture of much clearness and force.'—*Globe.*

'A notable sketch, at once scholarly and interesting.'—*English Mail.*

'No one is better qualified than Mr. Stanley Lane-Poole to take up the history and to depict the character of the last of the great Mogul monarchs.... Aurangzíb's career is ever a fascinating study.'—*Home News.*

'The author gives a description of the famous city of Sháh Jahán, its palaces, and the ceremonies and pageants of which they were the scene. ... Mr. Lane-Poole's well-written monograph presents all the most distinctive features of Aurangzíb's character and career.'—*Morning Post.*

MAJOR ROSS OF BLADENSBURG'S 'MARQUESS OF HASTINGS.'

'Major Ross of Bladensburg treats his subject skilfully and attractively, and his biography of Lord Hastings worthily sustains the high reputation of the Series in which it appears.'—*The Times.*

'This monograph is entitled to rank with the best of the Series, the compiler having dealt capably and even brilliantly with his materials.' —*English Mail.*

'Instinct with interest.'—*Glasgow Evening News.*

'As readable as it is instructive.'—*Globe.*

'A truly admirable monograph.'—*Glasgow Herald.*

'Major Ross has done his work admirably, and bids fair to be one of the best writers the Army of our day has given to the country.... A most acceptable and entrancing little volume.'—*Daily Chronicle.*

'It is a volume that merits the highest praise. Major Ross of Bladensburg has represented Lord Hastings and his work in India in the right light, faithfully described the country as it was, and in a masterly manner makes one realize how important was the period covered by this volume.'—*Manchester Courier.*

'This excellent monograph ought not to be overlooked by any one who would fully learn the history of British rule in India.'—*Manchester Examiner.*

Opinions of the Press

ON

COLONEL MALLESON'S 'DUPLEIX.'

'In the character of Dupleix there was the element of greatness that contact with India seems to have generated in so many European minds, French as well as English, and a broad capacity for government, which, if suffered to have full play, might have ended in giving the whole of Southern India to France. Even as it was, Colonel Malleson shows how narrowly the prize slipped from French grasp. In 1783 the Treaty of Versailles arrived just in time to save the British power from extinction.'—*Times.*

'One of the best of Sir W. Hunter's interesting and valuable series. Colonel Malleson writes out of the fulness of familiarity, moving with ease over a field which he had long ago surveyed in every nook and corner. To do a small book as well as this on Dupleix has been done, will be recognised by competent judges as no small achievement. When one considers the bulk of the material out of which the little volume has been distilled, one can still better appreciate the labour and dexterity involved in the performance.'—*Academy.*

'A most compact and effective history of the French in India in a little handbook of 180 pages.'—*Nonconformist.*

'Well arranged, lucid and eminently readable, an excellent addition to a most useful series.'—*Record.*

COLONEL MALLESON'S 'AKBAR.'

'Colonel Malleson's interesting monograph on Akbar in the "Rulers of India" (Clarendon Press) should more than satisfy the general reader. Colonel Malleson traces the origin and foundation of the Mughal Empire; and, as an introduction to the history of Muhammadan India, the book leaves nothing to be desired.'—*St. James's Gazette.*

'This volume will, no doubt, be welcomed, even by experts in Indian history, in the light of a new, clear, and terse rendering of an old, but not worn-out theme. It is a worthy and valuable addition to Sir W. Hunter's promising series.'—*Athenæum.*

'Colonel Malleson has broken ground new to the general reader. The story of Akbar is briefly but clearly told, with an account of what he was and what he did, and how he found and how he left India.... The native chronicles of the reign are many, and from them it is still possible, as Colonel Malleson has shown, to construct a living portrait of this great and mighty potentate.'—*Scots Observer.*

'The brilliant historian of the Indian Mutiny has been assigned in this volume of the series an important epoch and a strong personality for critical study, and he has admirably fulfilled his task.... Alike in dress and style, this volume is a fit companion for its predecessor.'—*Manchester Guardian.*

Opinions of the Press
ON
CAPTAIN TROTTER'S 'WARREN HASTINGS.'

'The publication, recently noticed in this place, of the "Letters, Despatches, and other State Papers preserved in the Foreign Department of the Government of India, 1772–1785," has thrown entirely new light from the most authentic sources on the whole history of Warren Hastings and his government of India. Captain L. J. Trotter's WARREN HASTINGS is accordingly neither inopportune nor devoid of an adequate raison d'être. Captain Trotter is well known as a competent and attractive writer on Indian history, and this is not the first time that Warren Hastings has supplied him with a theme.'—*The Times.*

'He has put his best work into this memoir.... His work is of distinct literary merit, and is worthy of a theme than which British history presents none nobler. It is a distinct gain to the British race to be enabled, as it now may, to count the great Governor-General among those heroes for whom it need not blush.'—*Scotsman.*

'Captain Trotter has done his work well, and his volume deserves to stand with that on Dalhousie by Sir William Hunter. Higher praise it would be hard to give it.'—*New York Herald.*

'Captain Trotter has done full justice to the fascinating story of the splendid achievements of a great Englishman.'—*Manchester Guardian.*

'A brief but admirable biography of the first Governor-General of India.'—*Newcastle Chronicle.*

'A book which all must peruse who desire to be "up to date" on the subject.'—*The Globe.*

MR. KEENE'S 'MADHAVA RAO SINDHIA.'

'Mr. Keene has the enormous advantage, not enjoyed by every producer of a book, of knowing intimately the topic he has taken up. He has compressed into these 203 pages an immense amount of information, drawn from the best sources, and presented with much neatness and effect.'—*The Globe.*

'Mr. Keene tells the story with knowledge and impartiality, and also with sufficient graphic power to make it thoroughly readable. The recognition of Sindhia in the "Rulers" series is just and graceful, and it cannot fail to give satisfaction to the educated classes of our Indian fellow-subjects.'—*North British Daily Mail.*

'The volume bears incontestable proofs of the expenditure of considerable research by the author, and sustains the reputation he had already acquired by his "Sketch of the History of Hindustan."'—*Freeman's Journal.*

'Among the eighteen rulers of India included in the scheme of Sir William Hunter only five are natives of India, and of these the great Madhoji Sindhia is, with the exception of Akbar, the most illustrious. Mr. H. G. Keene, a well-known and skilful writer on Indian questions, is fortunate in his subject, for the career of the greatest bearer of the historic name of Sindhia covered the exciting period from the capture of Delhi, the Imperial capital, by the Persian Nadir Shah, to the occupation of the same city by Lord Lake.... Mr. Keene gives a lucid description of his subsequent policy, especially towards the English when he was brought face to face with Warren Hastings.'—*The Daily Graphic.*

Opinions of the Press

ON

MAJOR-GENERAL SIR OWEN BURNE'S
'CLYDE AND STRATHNAIRN.'

'In "Clyde and Strathnairn," a contribution to Sir William Hunter's excellent "Rulers of India" series (Oxford, at the Clarendon Press), Sir Owen Burne gives a lucid sketch of the military history of the Indian Mutiny and its suppression by the two great soldiers who give their names to his book. The space is limited for so large a theme, but Sir Owen Burne skilfully adjusts his treatment to his limits, and rarely violates the conditions of proportion imposed upon him.' . . . 'Sir Owen Burne does not confine himself exclusively to the military narrative. He gives a brief sketch of the rise and progress of the Mutiny, and devotes a chapter to the Reconstruction which followed its suppression.' . . . '— well written, well proportioned, and eminently worthy of the series to which it belongs.'—*The Times.*

'Sir Owen Burne who, by association, experience, and relations with one of these generals, is well qualified for the task, writes with knowledge, perspicuity, and fairness.'—*Saturday Review.*

'As a brief record of a momentous epoch in India this little book is a remarkable piece of clear, concise, and interesting writing.'—*The Colonies and India.*

'Sir Owen Burne has written this book carefully, brightly, and with excellent judgement, and we in India cannot read such a book without feeling that he has powerfully aided the accomplished editor of the series in a truly patriotic enterprise.'—*Bombay Gazette.*

'The volume on "Clyde and Strathnairn" has just appeared, and proves to be a really valuable addition to the series. Considering its size and the extent of ground it covers it is one of the best books about the Indian Mutiny of which we know.'—*Englishman.*

'Sir Owen Burne, who has written the latest volume for Sir William Hunter's "Rulers of India" series, is better qualified than any living person to narrate, from a military standpoint, the story of the suppression of the Indian Mutiny.'—*Daily Telegraph.*

'Sir Owen Burne's book on "Clyde and Strathnairn" is worthy to rank with the best in the admirable series to which it belongs.'—*Manchester Examiner.*

'The book is admirably written; and there is probably no better sketch, equally brief, of the stirring events with which it deals.'—*Scotsman.*

'Sir Owen Burne, from the part he played in the Indian Mutiny, and from his long connexion with the Government of India, and from the fact that he was military secretary of Lord Strathnairn both in India and in Ireland, is well qualified for the task which he has undertaken.'—*The Athenæum.*

Opinions of the Press

ON

VISCOUNT HARDINGE'S 'LORD HARDINGE.'

'An exception to the rule that biographies ought not to be entrusted to near relatives. Lord Hardinge, a scholar and an artist, has given us an accurate record of his father's long and distinguished services. There is no filial exaggeration. The author has dealt with some controversial matters with skill, and has managed to combine truth with tact and regard for the feelings of others.'—*The Saturday Review.*

'This interesting life reveals the first Lord Hardinge as a brave, just, able man, the very soul of honour, admired and trusted equally by friends and political opponents. The biographer . . . has produced a most engaging volume, which is enriched by many private and official documents that have not before seen the light.'—*The Anti-Jacobin.*

'Lord Hardinge has accomplished a grateful, no doubt, but, from the abundance of material and delicacy of certain matters, a very difficult task in a workmanlike manner, marked by restraint and lucidity.'—*The Pall Mall Gazette.*

'His son and biographer has done his work with a true appreciation of proportion, and has added substantially to our knowledge of the Sutlej Campaign.'—*Vanity Fair.*

'The present Lord Hardinge is in some respects exceptionally well qualified to tell the tale of the eventful four years of his father's Governor-Generalship.'—*The Times.*

'It contains a full account of everything of importance in Lord Hardinge's military and political career; it is arranged . . . so as to bring into special prominence his government of India; and it gives a lifelike and striking picture of the man.'—*Academy.*

'The style is clear, the treatment dispassionate, and the total result a manual which does credit to the interesting series in which it figures.'—*The Globe.*

'The concise and vivid account which the son has given of his father's career will interest many readers.'—*The Morning Post.*

'Eminently readable for everybody. The history is given succinctly, and the unpublished letters quoted are of real value.'—*The Colonies and India.*

'Compiled from public documents, family papers, and letters, this brief biography gives the reader a clear idea of what Hardinge was, both as a soldier and as an administrator.'—*The Manchester Examiner.*

'An admirable sketch.'—*The New York Herald.*

'The Memoir is well and concisely written, and is accompanied by an excellent likeness after the portrait by Sir Francis Grant.'—*The Queen.*

Opinions of the Press
ON
SIR HENRY CUNNINGHAM'S 'EARL CANNING.'

'Sir Henry Cunningham's rare literary skill and his knowledge of Indian life and affairs are not now displayed for the first time, and he has enjoyed exceptional advantages in dealing with his present subject. Lord Granville, Canning's contemporary at school and colleague in public life and one of his oldest friends, furnished his biographer with notes of his recollections of the early life of his friend. Sir Henry Cunningham has also been allowed access to the Diary of Canning's private secretary, to the Journal of his military secretary, and to an interesting correspondence between the Governor-General and his great lieutenant, Lord Lawrence.'—*The Times.*

'Sir H. S. Cunningham has succeeded in writing the history of a critical period in so fair and dispassionate a manner as to make it almost a matter of astonishment that the motives which he has so clearly grasped should ever have been misinterpreted, and the results which he indicates so grossly misjudged. Nor is the excellence of his work less conspicuous from the literary than from the political and historical point of view.'—*Glasgow Herald.*

'Sir H. S. Cunningham has treated his subject adequately. In vivid language he paints his word-pictures, and with calm judicial analysis he also proves himself an able critic of the actualities, causes, and results of the outbreak, also a temperate, just appreciator of the character and policy of Earl Canning.'—*The Court Journal.*

REV. W. H. HUTTON'S 'MARQUESS WELLESLEY.'

'Mr. Hutton has brought to his task an open mind, a trained historical judgement, and a diligent study of a great body of original material. Hence he is enabled to present a true, authentic, and original portrait of one of the greatest of Anglo-Indian statesmen, doing full justice to his military policy and achievements, and also to his statesmanlike efforts for the organization and consolidation of that Empire which he did so much to sustain.'—*Times.*

'To the admirable candour and discrimination which characterize Mr. Hutton's monograph as an historical study must be added the literary qualities which distinguish it and make it one of the most readable volumes of the series. The style is vigorous and picturesque, and the arrangement of details artistic in its just regard for proportion and perspective. In short, there is no point of view from which the work deserves anything but praise.'—*Glasgow Herald.*

'The Rev. W. H. Hutton has done his work well, and achieves with force and lucidity the task he sets himself: to show how, under Wellesley, the Indian company developed and ultimately became the supreme power in India. To our thinking his estimate of this great statesman is most just.'—*Black and White.*

'Mr. Hutton has told the story of Lord Wellesley's life in an admirable manner, and has provided a most readable book.'—*Manchester Examiner.*

'Mr. Hutton's range of information is wide, his division of subjects appropriate, and his diction scholarly and precise.'—*Saturday Review.*

Opinions of the Press

ON

SIR LEPEL GRIFFIN'S 'RANJIT SINGH.'

'We can thoroughly praise Sir Lepel Griffin's work as an accurate and appreciative account of the beginnings and growth of the Sikh religion and of the temporal power founded upon it by a strong and remorseless chieftain.'—*The Times.*

'Sir Lepel Griffin treats his topic with thorough mastery, and his account of the famous Mahárájá and his times is, consequently, one of the most valuable as well as interesting volumes of the series of which it forms a part.'—*The Globe.*

'From first to last it is a model of what such a work should be, and a classic.'—*The St. Stephen's Review.*

'The monograph could not have been entrusted to more capable hands than those of Sir Lepel Griffin, who spent his official life in the Punjaub.'—*The Scotsman.*

'At once the shortest and best history of the rise and fall of the Sikh monarchy.'—*The North British Daily Mail.*

'Not only a biography of the Napoleon of the East, but a luminous picture of his country; the chapter on Sikh Theocracy being a notable example of compact thought.'—*The Liverpool Mercury.*

MR. DEMETRIUS BOULGER'S 'LORD WILLIAM BENTINCK.'

'The " Rulers of India" series has received a valuable addition in the biography of the late Lord William Bentinck. The subject of this interesting memoir was a soldier as well as a statesman. He was mainly instrumental in bringing about the adoption of the overland route and in convincing the people of India that a main factor in English policy was a disinterested desire for their welfare. Lord William's despatches and minutes, several of which are textually reproduced in Mr. Boulger's praiseworthy little book, display considerable literary skill and are one and all State papers of signal worth.'—*Daily Telegraph.*

'Mr. Boulger is no novice in dealing with Oriental history and Oriental affairs, and in the career of Lord William Bentinck he has found a theme very much to his taste, which he treats with adequate knowledge and literary skill.'—*The Times.*

'Mr. Boulger writes clearly and well, and his volume finds an accepted place in the very useful and informing series which Sir William Wilson Hunter is editing so ably.'—*Independent.*

Opinions of the Press

ON

MR. J. S. COTTON'S 'MOUNTSTUART ELPHINSTONE.'

'Sir William Hunter, the editor of the series to which this book belongs, was happily inspired when he entrusted the Life of Elphinstone, one of the most scholarly of Indian rulers, to Mr. Cotton, who, himself a scholar of merit and repute, is brought by the nature of his daily avocations into close and constant relations with scholars. . . . We live in an age in which none but specialists can afford to give more time to the memoirs of even the most distinguished Anglo-Indians than will be occupied by reading Mr. Cotton's two hundred pages. He has performed his task with great skill and good sense. This is just the kind of Life of himself which the wise, kindly, high-souled man, who is the subject of it, would read with pleasure in the Elysian Fields.'—Sir M. E. Grant Duff, in *The Academy*.

'To so inspiring a theme few writers are better qualified to do ample justice than the author of "The Decennial Statement of the Moral and Material Progress and Condition of India." Sir T. Colebrooke's larger biography of Elphinstone appeals mainly to Indian specialists, but Mr. Cotton's slighter sketch is admirably adapted to satisfy the growing demand for a knowledge of Indian history and of the personalities of Anglo-Indian statesmen which Sir William Hunter has done so much to create.'—*The Times*.

DR. BRADSHAW'S 'SIR THOMAS MUNRO.'

'A most valuable, compact and interesting memoir for those looking forward to or engaged in the work of Indian administration.'—*Scotsman*.

'It is a careful and sympathetic survey of a life which should always serve as an example to the Indian soldier and civilian.'—*Yorkshire Post*.

'A true and vivid record of Munro's life-work in almost autobiographical form.'—*Glasgow Herald*.

'Of the work before us we have nothing but praise. The story of Munro's career in India is in itself of exceptional interest and importance.'—*Freeman's Journal*.

'The work could not have been better done; it is a monument of painstaking care, exhaustive research, and nice discrimination.'—*People*.

'This excellent and spirited little monograph catches the salient points of Munro's career, and supplies some most valuable quotations from his writings and papers.'—*Manchester Guardian*.

'It would be impossible to imagine a more attractive and at the same time instructive book about India.'—*Liverpool Courier*.

'It is one of the best volumes of this excellent series.'—*Imperial and Asiatic Quarterly Review*.

'The book throughout is arranged in an admirably clear manner and there is evident on every page a desire for truth, and nothing but the truth.'—*Commerce*.

'A clear and scholarly piece of work.'—*Indian Journal of Education*.

Opinions of the Press

ON

MR. MORSE STEPHENS' 'ALBUQUERQUE.'

'Mr. Stephens' able and instructive monograph... We may commend Mr. Morse Stephens' volume, both as an adequate summary of an important period in the history of the relations between Asia and Europe, and as a suggestive treatment of the problem of why Portugal failed and England succeeded in founding an Indian Empire.'—*The Times.*

'Mr. H. Morse Stephens has made a very readable book out of the foundation of the Portuguese power in India. According to the practice of the series to which it belongs it is called a life of Affonso de Albuquerque, but the Governor is only the central and most important figure in a brief history of the Portuguese in the East down to the time when the Dutch and English intruded on their preserves... A pleasantly-written and trustworthy book on an interesting man and time.'—*The Saturday Review.*

'Mr. Morse Stephens' *Albuquerque* is a solid piece of work, well put together, and full of interest.'—*The Athenæum.*

'Mr. Morse Stephens' studies in Indian and Portuguese history have thoroughly well qualified him for approaching the subject... He has presented the facts of Albuquerque's career, and sketched the events marking the rule of his predecessor Almeida, and of his immediate successors in the Governorship and Viceroyalty of India in a compact, lucid, and deeply interesting form.'—*The Scotsman.*

SIR CHARLES AITCHISON'S 'LORD LAWRENCE.'

'No man knows the policy, principles, and character of John Lawrence better than Sir Charles Aitchison. The salient features and vital principles of his work as a ruler, first in the Punjab, and afterwards as Viceroy, are set forth with remarkable clearness.'—*Scotsman.*

'A most admirable sketch of the great work done by Sir John Lawrence, who not only ruled India, but saved it.'—*Manchester Examiner.*

'Sir Charles Aitchison's narrative is uniformly marked by directness, order, clearness, and grasp; it throws additional light into certain nooks of Indian affairs; and it leaves upon the mind a very vivid and complete impression of Lord Lawrence's vigorous, resourceful, discerning, and valiant personality.'—*Newcastle Daily Chronicle.*

'Sir Charles knows the Punjab thoroughly, and has made this little book all the more interesting by his account of the Punjab under John Lawrence and his subordinates.'—*Yorkshire Post.*

Opinions of the Press
ON
LEWIN BENTHAM BOWRING'S 'HAIDAR ALÍ AND TIPÚ SULTÁN.'

'Mr. Bowring's portraits are just, and his narrative of the continuous military operations of the period full and accurate.'—*Times.*

'The story has been often written, but never better or more concisely than here, where the father and son are depicted vividly and truthfully "in their habit as they lived." There is not a volume of the whole series which is better done than this, or one which shows greater insight.'—*Daily Chronicle.*

'Mr. Bowring has been well chosen to write this memorable history, because he has had the best means of collecting it, having himself formerly been Chief Commissioner of Mysore. The account of the Mysore war is well done, and Mr. Bowring draws a stirring picture of our determined adversary.'—*Army and Navy Gazette.*

'An excellent example of compression and precision. Many volumes might be written about the long war in Mysore, and we cannot but admire the skill with which Mr. Bowring has condensed the history of the struggle. His book is as terse and concise as a book can be.'—*North British Daily Mail.*

'Mr. Bowring's book is one of the freshest and best of a series most valuable to all interested in the concerns of the British Empire in the East.'—*English Mail.*

'The story of the final capture of Seringapatam is told with skill and graphic power by Mr. Bowring, who throughout the whole work shows himself a most accurate and interesting historian.'—*Perthshire Advertiser.*

COLONEL MALLESON'S 'LORD CLIVE.'

'This book gives a spirited and accurate sketch of a very extraordinary personality.'—*Speaker.*

'Colonel Malleson writes a most interesting account of Clive's great work in India—so interesting that, having begun to read it, one is unwilling to lay it aside until the last page has been reached. The character of Clive as a leader of men, and especially as a cool, intrepid, and resourceful general, is ably described; and at the same time the author never fails to indicate the far-reaching political schemes which inspired the valour of Clive and laid the foundation of our Indian Empire.'—*North British Daily Mail.*

'This monograph is admirably written by one thoroughly acquainted and in love with his subject.'—*Glasgow Herald.*

'No one is better suited than Colonel Malleson to write on Clive, and he has performed his task with distinct success. The whole narrative is, like everything Colonel Malleson writes, clear and full of vigour.'—*Yorkshire Post.*

'Colonel Malleson is reliable and fair, and the especial merit of his book is that it always presents a clear view of the whole of the vast theatre in which Clive gradually produces such an extraordinary change of scene.'—*Newcastle Daily Chronicle.*

Opinions of the Press

ON

CAPT. TROTTER'S 'EARL OF AUCKLAND.'

'A vivid account of the causes, conduct, and consequences of "the costly, fruitless, and unrighteous" Afghan War of 1838.'—*St. James's Gazette.*

'To write such a monograph was a thankless task, but it has been accomplished with entire success by Captain L. J. Trotter. He has dealt calmly and clearly with Lord Auckland's policy, domestic and military, with its financial results, and with the general tendency of Lord Auckland's rule.'—*Yorkshire Post.*

'To this distressing story (of the First Afghan War) Captain Trotter devotes the major portion of his pages. He tells it well and forcibly; but is drawn, perhaps unavoidably, into the discussion of many topics of controversy which, to some readers, may seem to be hardly as yet finally decided. . . . It is only fair to add that two chapters are devoted to "Lord Auckland's Domestic Policy," and to his relations with "The Native States of India".'—*The Times.*

'Captain Trotter's *Earl of Auckland* is a most interesting book, and its excellence as a condensed, yet luminous, history of the first Afghan War deserves warm recognition.'—*Scotsman.*

'It points a moral which our Indian Rulers cannot afford to forget so long as they still have Russia and Afghanistan to count with.'—*Glasgow Herald.*

Supplementary Volume: price 3s. 6d.

'JAMES THOMASON,' BY SIR RICHARD TEMPLE.

'Sir R. Temple's book possesses a high value as a dutiful and interesting memorial of a man of lofty ideals, whose exploits were none the less memorable because achieved exclusively in the field of peaceful administration.'—*Times.*

'It is the peculiar distinction of this work that it interests a reader less in the official than in the man himself.'—*Scotsman.*

'This is a most interesting book: to those who know India, and knew the man, it is of unparalleled interest, but no one who has the Imperial instinct which has taught the English to rule subject races "for their own welfare" can fail to be struck by the simple greatness of this character.'—*Pall Mall Gazette.*

'Mr. Thomason was a great Indian statesman. He systematized the revenue system of the North-West Provinces, and improved every branch of the administration. He was remarkable, like many great Indians, for the earnestness of his religious faith, and Sir Richard Temple brings this out in an admirable manner.'—*British Weekly.*

'The book is "a portrait drawn by the hand of affection," of one whose life was "a pattern of how a Christian man ought to live." Special prominence is given to the religious aspects of Mr. Thomason's character, and the result is a very readable biographical sketch.'—*Christian.*

Opinions of the Press

ON

SIR AUCKLAND COLVIN'S 'JOHN RUSSELL COLVIN.'

'The concluding volume of Sir William Hunter's admirable "Rulers of India" series is devoted to a biography of John Russell Colvin. Mr. Colvin, as private secretary to Lord Auckland, the Governor-General during the first Afghan War, and as Lieutenant-Governor of the North-West Provinces during the Mutiny, bore a prominent part in the government of British India at two great crises of its history. His biographer is his son, Sir Auckland Colvin, who does full justice to his father's career and defends him stoutly against certain allegations which have passed into history.... It is a valuable and effective contribution to an admirable series. In style and treatment of its subject it is well worthy of its companions.'—*Times.*

'Sir Auckland Colvin has been able to throw new light on many of the acts of Lord Auckland's administration, and on the state of affairs at Agra on the outbreak of the Mutiny.... This memoir will serve to recall the splendid work which Colvin really performed in India, and to exhibit him as a thoroughly honourable man and conscientious ruler.'—*Daily Telegraph.*

'This book gives an impressive account of Colvin's public services, his wide grasp of native affairs, and the clean-cut policy which marked his tenure of power.'—*Leeds Mercury.*

'The story of John Colvin's career indicates the lines on which the true history of the first Afghan War and of the Indian Mutiny should be written.... Not only has the author been enabled to make use of new and valuable material, but he has also constructed therefrom new and noteworthy explanations of the position of affairs at two turning-points in Indian history.'—*Academy.*

'High as is the standard of excellence attained by the volumes of this series, Sir Auckland Colvin's earnest work has reached the high-water mark.'—*Army and Navy Gazette.*

'Sir Auckland Colvin has done his part with great tact and skill. As an example of the clear-sighted way in which he treats the various Indian problems we may cite what he says on the education of the natives—a question always of great moment to the subject of this biography.'—*Manchester Guardian.*

'Sir Auckland Colvin gives us an admirable study of his subject, both as a man of affairs and as a student in private life. In doing this, his picturesque theme allows him, without outstepping the biographical limits assigned, to present graphic pictures of old Calcutta and Indian life in general.'—*Manchester Courier.*

'This little volume contains pictures of India, past and present, which it would be hard to match for artistic touch and fine feeling. We wish there were more of the same kind to follow.'—*St. James's Gazette.*

'The monograph is a valuable addition to a series of which we have more than once pointed out the utility and the excellence.'—*Glasgow Herald.*

www.ingramcontent.com/pod-product-compliance
Lightning Source LLC
Chambersburg PA
CBHW022017220426
43663CB00007B/1111